What Your Clients Won't Tell You

ISBN:0-9665438-1-5

Published by Tenacity Inc., Roswell, Georgia
www.tenacity.com
Cover design by Jodi Berlin

Tenacity Incorporated

For Karen, Kimberly, Kristin and Missy Leigh.
Thanks for believing in me.

Acknowledgments

I recognize that without the help of others this book would never have been written. I'd like to thank:

Bill Edmundson, who gave me the opportunity to begin this journey.

Kate Ravin, who suggested I write the book and who worked tirelessly on editing its content.

David Murphy, for the last push that made this possible.

My partners Chris McCarthy and Steve Wurzbacher for their faith, trust, insight and encouragement.

Kim Gamble, Bob Rasmussen, Mike Bendinelli, Dennis Good, and Brad Linden for reading the manuscript and offering their advice and insights.

To everyone—past and present—in ARAMARK's Healthcare Support Services division. Special thanks to John Farquharson, Connie Girard di-Carlo, Gerry Ehrlich, Ed Kelly, Dick Morgan, Greg Ross, Ivon English, Marte Shadis, Alan Crowell, John Sagendorf, Walt Geggis, Dick Jack, Bill Wolf, Carl Marsalis, Keith Cullinan, Mary Beth Crimmins, John Brady, Bryon Hotzler, Bonnie Duckworth, Dottie Page, Craig Stretch, Carol Carlson and Bob Gray.

And finally, to Jack Hoffman—one of the best "multi-unit managers" I've ever worked with.

Foreword

This book is the midpoint of a journey undertaken at my behest almost ten years ago with a midnight ride down I-95 from Pennsylvania to South Carolina. Luckily, John Gamble and Steve Wurzbacher (then my VP's of Marketing and Sales) were fully equipped with cruise control and radar detector because time was short and they were fervently pursuing a mission. The mission they shared, which at that time was an absolute business imperative, was to get inside the hearts and minds of *former* clients. You see, even though Steve's sales team had been succeeded in breaking a long standing company record by selling $42 million in new business that year, we had lost $40 million of existing business during the same period. John's assignment was to understand where our organization had failed and to learn from our former clients' insights and perceptions. It was clear to all of us that if we couldn't stop client defections, our new business efforts—no matter how successful—would be in vain.

For my friend, John Gamble, that three-day trip was the embryo of his career as one of this nation's leading client retention consultants. And, though currently serving at the helm of a new company, I'm a Clients for Life believer more than ever. For fellow executives who are truly committed to client stewardship through understanding and managing pivotal business relationships and, even more importantly, for those who believe they can and should retain every single one of those valuable clients, John's methods are revolutionary. For the first time, keeping your clients can be based on a sustainable process that actually enriches the association between firms.

As you read, it is important not to get hung up in the strict definition of the word "client" which appears in the title and is used throughout the body of the book. Whether you actually refer to them as clients or partners or even customers really does not matter. The process described will help you retain any business affiliation that involves significant effort and investment to acquire, is highly valued and has the potential to be of long term duration.

What Your Clients Won't Tell You... And Your Managers Don't Know is an easy read. Don't let that fool you, however. It is filled with exciting, high-impact principles that can be readily executed, measured, and sustained. Collectively, these principles represent incredible innovation and proactive strategic thinking in retaining and nurturing your firm's most critical asset—its clients.

One important cautionary note: While the concepts in the book seem very straightforward and logical, the implementation of this process requires a high degree of senior management commitment and courage. Courage, because the process involves outside, third-party input to get to the core of the issues affecting the firm's ability to retain its clients. Those people in an organization who are most threatened by objective, third-party involvement will resist taking the actions outlined. However, if management perseveres in implementing the processes detailed in this book, dramatic rewards in both client retention and organizational development can be realized.

So, whether you are closer to I-95 or I-5, this book can be the beginning of an exciting journey in making your business better. It is a guidepost to effectively understanding and managing the most important part of your business… your clients.

—Bill Edmundson
Chief Executive Officer
The Wood Company
Allentown, Pennsylvania
June 1,1995

Introduction

This book was written to assist the professional manager whose livelihood depends on selling and retaining *clients*.

In my experience, there is a profound difference between a "client" and a "customer." While there is no doubt that retaining customers is critical to the owner of a restaurant or auto parts store, the loss of any one customer isn't likely to affect the viability of the business.

In contrast, when an advertising agency, management services firm or engineering company loses a client, the ramifications to its business can be significant. Consider the facts: a client's business is usually committed for years at a time—in effect, once the client decides to hire a provider of services, the client is "out of the market;" the service provided is so important that a lengthy, negotiated contract guides their delivery; these transactions involve six and often seven figure sums; employees at all levels of both organizations interact with one another on their firm's behalf; the decision to do business together often survives the people making that decision; and the decision to end the affiliation—which often requires as little as a 30 day cancellation clause—involves massive changes for both organizations.

As many of you have found, the "customer service" techniques trumpeted in books and seminars simply don't work in this environment. And trying to adapt Total Quality Management principles (TQM) designed for product-based operations can be even more frustrating. In fact, in my experience, TQM—with all of it's statistics, analysis, charts and reports—actually inhibits managers from taking the action required to protect their business.

While several books have drawn the distinction between selling to clients and selling to customers, none have dealt with the issue of client retention. To my knowledge, this is the first book dedicated to providing you with the strategies and tactics required to *keep* the clients you've worked so hard to get. It's based on ten years of experience with a wide variety of professional service organizations. The client-retention principles outlined are currently helping protect more than one billion dollars in service management contracts. They work—but only if you work at them.

To make these lessons come alive, I've written What Your Clients Won't Tell You…And Your Managers Don't Know as a story rather than a textbook. Although the characters are fictional, the questions they ask and the strategies they recommend come directly from actual situations.

I hope you'll empathize with Bonnie and learn from Jack—and that your involvement with them will help you cultivate profitable, satisfying relationships with your own clients.

When you're finished reading, I hope you'll conclude that this is "just plain, common sense." If that's your reaction, I'll be pleased and you'll be on your way to helping your organization prosper. After all, common sense is not always common practice.

Good luck!

John Gamble
June 1995

Contents

Afterword

John Gamble is the founder of Tenacity Incorporated and leads the firm's development efforts in finding and teaching more effective, productive and profitable ways to manage client retention for the long term.

Tenacity Incorporated and the Clients for Life® client retention process are currently protecting over $1 billion in service management contracts.

Tenacity Incorporated is headquartered in Atlanta, Georgia and is available to work with service management firms of all sizes in tailoring, implementing and imprinting into their culture, the practical aspects of the Clients for Life client retention process.

Please write to us at 550 Oakhaven Drive, Suite 2-B, Roswell, Georgia 30075 or call at (404) 642-0701.

The Clients for Life Philosophy

She was proud of being named as his successor. Proud but scared to death. She worried about filling the shoes of a "living legend." Her concerns didn't have anything to do with the technology or the managers she'd be responsible for. At this point in her career, the technical aspects of the job were no-brainers. And she'd always felt pride in being known as a "people person." She didn't think she'd have any problems within the organization. But she didn't know how she was going to live up to the standard he'd set with the clients.

She was anxious about beginning work on the transition, so she arrived a few minutes early for their first appointment. His secretary, Rosemary, greeted her warmly and escorted her to his office. The room was amazingly uncluttered. The only prominent thing on his desk was a rather large, hand-carved wooden paper weight that read: "Attitude and Action." She couldn't help but think how different his desk was from hers. It wasn't uncommon for her to have so many charts and financial comparisons on her desk that its surface disappeared.

"Not much going on?" she asked Rosemary. "Far from it," Rosemary replied. "The competition is making a play for our largest account. They've underbid us by eight percent on the new contract. And the account manager has just decided to accept a position in the Far East. But, Mr. Henderson is on top of things, so I wouldn't worry."

Rosemary turned and walked toward the door. As she left the office she said, "If I can get you anything, just let me know."

The thought "How about a bottle of Excedrin?" crossed Bonnie's mind. Underbid by eight percent on their largest account, and losing the manager at the same time! The only thing she couldn't figure out was why Rosemary seemed so calm. Where Bonnie came from, this was a crisis.

Just as a thousand and one things raced through her mind, he walked in. She still marveled at how small he was. His size just didn't fit the image of a corporate legend. But his lack of physical stature faded as he held out his hand and smiled the biggest smile she'd seen in a long time.

"I'm glad you're here," he said. "I've been eager to begin the transition."

"Same here," she said. "But it looks as if I'm arriving at the worst time possible."

"What do you mean?" Jack asked.

"Rosemary just told me what's happening. Being underbid by eight percent and having the manager leave is not the welcome I'd hoped for."

"I see you're concerned about the situation, but I'm confident things will work out," Jack responded.

"I wish I had your confidence," Bonnie replied. "Somehow, these things have a way of escalating out of control. And the last thing I need is to lose a major account the month after you retire. It's going to be tough enough to carry on your legacy. You haven't lost an account in over seven years. And now it looks as if I'll have one on the ropes the first month you're gone."

"My legacy?!" Jack laughed quietly to himself.

"Bonnie, we're not going to lose this account. We've

already taken care of that."

" You mean we've put in a lower bid?"

"No, in fact, I was there this morning reviewing proposals with our client. The competition has put in a bid that's seven to eight percent lower than ours."

"Well, then, how can you say we're not going to lose the account? Seven to eight percent is a lot of money these days."

"Yes, it is. But bid price is rarely the only consideration. And besides, we know that we retained the account yesterday."

"You mean they signed the new contract with us?" asked Bonnie.

"No, not exactly," Jack responded.

"Well then, I'm afraid you lost me. How could we have retained the account if they didn't sign the new contract?"

Jack could tell by the exasperated look on Bonnie's face

that she didn't know about the Clients for Life® client retention process. And for a brief moment, he felt her anxiety and fear.

"Bonnie," he asked, "what's your philosophy on retaining clients?"

"Simple… whenever the contract is due for renewal, we do whatever it takes to retain the business!" she answered.

"When the contract is due for renewal? Just when is that?"

Bonnie was getting more confused by the minute and just a little irritated by such a basic question. But Jack's smile made him hard to be angry with. Besides, wasn't it obvious that the contract was due for renewal on its expiration date?

"Jack," she said, "unless I'm missing something, the contract is due for renewal on the expiration date it stipulates."

"And you'd do anything to renew it?" Jack asked.

"Anything! Anything legal and moral, that is," she added.

"Hmm... interesting."

"Why is that?" Bonnie responded. "That's pretty basic, isn't it?"

"Most people would think so," Jack said, "but we do things a little differently around here."

Bonnie knew Jack wasn't kidding. His philosophies were unique, and she hoped these meetings would allow her to find out his secrets to client retention. After all, he had the best client retention record in the company, if not the industry. And from painful personal experience, she knew what happened when a key client was lost.

Just then, Jack said, "I know we have a lot to accomplish over the next few days, and I'd like to begin by sharing the lessons we've learned about retaining clients."

She couldn't believe it. "I'm all ears," she said. "I can't wait to hear your secrets."

"Secrets?" Jack chuckled. "No, Bonnie, they're not secrets at all. In fact, if every one of my managers can't tell you everything I'm about to reveal, then I've failed to prepare them properly."

"Then why don't all the district managers in the division use your methods?" Bonnie asked.

Jack looked into her eyes and knew she needed to hear the truth. After all, in less than three weeks she'd be assuming responsibility for everyone and everything that mattered to him from a business standpoint.

"Bonnie," he said, "once we began having a bit of success retaining clients, everyone wanted to know what we were doing. They all came looking for the quick fix. Everyone wanted the magic pill that would make everything OK between them and their clients."

"I know what you mean," she said. "Everyone's under tremendous pressure to improve the bottom line. Any program that will help do that gets a lot of attention."

"But that's just it!" Jack nearly shouted. "What I'm about to share with you isn't a 'program.' It's not something you start and stop. It's an ongoing commitment you make to your clients and people."

Bonnie could sense that Jack's words expressed his most deeply held values.

"Bonnie, our philosophy is simple," Jack continued. "It's all about focusing on current clients as the key to profitable growth. But please don't assume that because this premise is simple, the process is simplistic. It isn't. Our philosophy is powerful."

"And I won't mislead you," Jack continued, "it takes guts to implement. Not that it requires a huge budget. It doesn't. However, it does require your time, courage, and commitment."

"Most things that really make a difference usually do...don't you agree?" he concluded.

Bonnie didn't quite know what to say, so she simply nodded her agreement.

"You see, Bonnie, most businesses believe growth comes from the next client. Later I'll explain the problems inherent in this thinking. And..."

Jack suddenly realized that he was starting to preach. This tendency of his was a source of amusement and pride among his managers. They all knew that when it came to discussing Clients for Life, Jack just couldn't help himself.

"I'm sorry for getting up on the soap box; please forgive me." Jack said. "But I've seen this philosophy make such a difference that I can't help but get excited about it."

Bonnie smiled. "Look Jack," she said, "you don't have anything to apologize for. I came here to learn why you've been so successful at retaining clients."

Jack had hoped she'd feel that way and was thrilled to hear her say so. He smiled and said, "OK, then let me get back to your question of 'Why don't the other District Managers use our philosophy?'"

He leaned back in his chair, looked Bonnie in the eye, and began.

"They all came searching for instant success. Rarely did any DM who asked for help acknowledge the time it takes to build an organizational culture that's focused on client retention."

What Your Clients Won't Tell You...
And Your Managers Don't Know

Bonnie listened intently as Jack continued.

"But, because we were having such success, they felt compelled to try the Clients for Life philosophy. So they took notes and learned enough to get their people all charged up—then they began making commitments to their clients."

"What happened?" Bonnie asked.

"Nothing, they shelved Clients for Life when they didn't have instant success and continued their search for the magic pill," Jack replied.

"That's unfortunate," Bonnie responded.

"What's unfortunate is that they didn't have the tenacity to stick with the process," Jack replied. "Because the Clients for Life philosophy is what they were looking for."

"Well Jack," Bonnie said, grabbing the armrests of her chair, "I'm not leaving until you tell me everything I need to know to follow in your footsteps!" They both chuckled.

Somehow Jack knew his people and clients would be in good hands with this woman. He liked her. But more important, she seemed genuinely interested in learning about the Clients for Life philosophy.

"Great!" he said. "Let me get you something to drink, and I'll begin at the beginning. Would you prefer coffee or a Coke®?"

The Cornerstones of Client Retention

Rosemary brought the coffee they'd asked for and closed the door. Cradling the warm cup, Bonnie said, "OK, Jack, tell me more about this simple philosophy of yours."

Jack smiled, took a sip of his coffee, and replied, "it all comes down to Attitude and Action."

As Jack spoke, Bonnie couldn't help but look at the paper weight on his desk.

"What do you mean, Jack?" she asked.

"Simply this: Once you decide to do business with a client you must have the attitude that you will keep that business forever. You'll be proactive in solving the clients' problems and assisting them in taking advantage of opportunities. And, when and if you perceive a threat to retaining the business, you will take whatever action is necessary to remove that threat."

"Attitude and Action are the cornerstones of our philosophies," Jack affirmed.

"Having an attitude that you won't lose clients is great," Bonnie replied. "But how does your attitude stop a client from canceling a contract?"

"It doesn't," Jack said. "Remember, Bonnie, I said it took Attitude and Action. But just the same, having the attitude I just mentioned is critical. And encouraging your people to have this attitude permeate the organization takes time. You see, your people have to believe you really mean it. They have to experience your commitment to the Clients for Life philosophy."

As Jack looked at Bonnie, he could see that she was beginning to process his ideas.

"For instance, Bonnie, how many times have you seen a situation in which a client canceled the contract and the management team rationalized the loss?"

Bonnie knew exactly what Jack meant but decided not to say anything. Anyway, she could sense that Jack really wasn't looking for an answer.

"You've heard the excuses just like I have... " Jack began

to recite them from memory. "'We never should have taken that client to begin with.' 'I'm glad they're gone; we weren't making any money.' 'Boy, was that place in the boondocks.' 'Great! Now we can reassign the management team to a larger account.' 'They were never worth the trouble they caused us...'"

Jack could have gone on, but from the look on Bonnie's face, he knew he'd made his point.

"Did I miss any?" Jack asked.

"I could probably add a few," Bonnie said, "but I hear you. In every one of these examples, management talked as if it didn't matter that the client had canceled the contract. In fact, in a few of your examples, management seemed relieved—even happy."

"Right!" Jack said. "And how long do you think the people will believe the organization's committed to client retention when they hear the senior managers talk like this?"

"Not long, I guess," Bonnie replied. "But Jack, everyone knows that some clients just don't work out?"

From Bonnie's tone, Jack could tell that Bonnie wasn't sure if she was asking a question or making a statement. His reply was quick. "Let me answer your question with a question. How would your people know which client losses to be concerned about and which clients are 'OK' to lose?"

Jack leaned back and let the question sink in.

Every answer that crossed Bonnie's mind had a hole in it. Finally she said, "I don't know Jack. How *do* you communicate that it's OK to lose one client but not another?"

"You don't!" he declared.

"We've learned that if management isn't concerned about every loss, their people are destined to get mixed messages."

"But aren't some clients more important than others?" Bonnie countered.

"Yes they are, Bonnie. We all have key clients. But relative importance is not the issue here. The issue is that all the clients we do business with should be crucial to us or we shouldn't be doing business with them."

Bonnie was mildly shocked by Jack's reply. It was the first time in her career she'd heard someone suggest *not* doing business with a client that wanted to do business.

By the look on Bonnie's face, Jack knew he had her attention. It was time to tell her the first of the components of the Clients for Life philosophy. He made sure he had eye contact and said, "Earlier you'd mentioned you hoped to hear about our 'secrets.' Here's the first and most important...

Client retention begins with the right clients under the right terms."

Jack waited until the words had sunk in and then said, "I told you our philosophy was simple."

Bonnie just stared at him. This was management 101. But Jack knew what she was thinking. He'd seen that look a hundred times before.

"Not the revelation you expected?" Jack asked, knowing he wouldn't wait for her answer. "If I were a betting man," he continued, "I'd make it even money that the power in what

I've just said hasn't hit you."

"You'd win that bet," Bonnie said, trying not to sound callous.

"Most people know that what I've just said is true," Jack acknowledged. "But few organizations actually implement the truths they know."

"You see, it's been our experience that dealing with the right clients under the right terms is the key to reducing lost business by more than fifty percent."

Bonnie was struck by how quickly Jack had become aware of her thoughts and concerns. It was as if he could read her mind.

Jack was now leaning forward and becoming more animated. "Think about it," he said. "How many times have you seen a contract signed, knowing it wasn't the right kind of business?"

Bonnie was about to reply, but Jack didn't give her time.

"Chances are, even though you knew it wasn't the 'right

business,' you convinced yourself that the potential profit was worth the risk. Am I correct?"

"I guess," Bonnie responded. "But what's your point? We all take advantage of opportunities that don't quite fit the mold."

"My point is this; what happened to that business?"

Jack had no intention of saying another word until Bonnie answered.

"Well, we kept some and lost some," Bonnie said after a few moments' reflection.

"And was the business you kept as profitable as you'd expected?" Jack asked quickly.

"If I were completely honest, I'd have to say 'no,'" Bonnie responded. "Those clients always took more time or effort than we anticipated. Even when it was a small account that we figured we could handle with little incremental effort, the problems seemed to consume us. In fact, those little 'add-on' accounts seem to cause more problems than our typical account."

Bonnie smiled at Jack and said, "I have a feeling this isn't the first time you've had this discussion."

Jack smiled back and replied, "No, it isn't. It took us years of listening to our own excuses before we realized that selecting our clients is one of the most important decisions a senior manager makes."

Jack spoke reflectively for the first time.

"Before we developed the Clients for Life philosophy, we failed to acknowledge that once we signed the contract, we committed ourselves and every person in our organization to meet the client's needs. And because we made some short-sighted decisions in the quest for immediate profit, we signed some contracts that created a lot of grief for our people. We put them in no-win situations. We let clients chew up our managers because we thought we could make a few extra bucks. The truth is," Jack continued, "if our financial people had ever allocated the true costs to those operations, it would have been clear we never earned a dime from any of them."

"But we learned," Jack continued. "Once we realized our

decisions had caused the problems, we made a commitment to everyone in the organization. We vowed never to take a client that didn't fit our criteria describing the ***right client under the right terms.***

"And that resulted in a fifty percent drop in lost business?" Bonnie asked.

"Actually, just a little better than fifty percent," Jack replied.

"Well Jack," Bonnie said, shaking her head, "if that one decision can prevent fifty percent of all the grief I've experienced from canceled contracts, you have my attention."

Jack smiled.

"Just one question," Bonnie added.

"Don't tell me," Jack said knowingly. "Who are the right clients and what are the right terms?"

By now, Bonnie was getting used to Jack's knack of anticipating her questions.

Jack reached for a binder that lay on the top of his credenza. He handed it to Bonnie and said, "The process we developed to answer that question is in this binder. Why don't you look it over while I refill your coffee?"

As the door closed behind Jack, Bonnie jotted down the most important ideas in a notebook she always carried. They read

I. The Clients for Life Philosophy

A. Client retention is not a "program"; it's an ongoing commitment to your clients and colleagues

II. Cornerstones of Client Retention

A. Attitude and Action are the cornerstones of the Clients for Life philosophy.

1. Attitude: We never lose a client that meets our criteria. We're proactive in helping the client solve problems and take advantage of opportunities.

2. Action: When and if we perceive a threat, we take whatever action is necessary to protect the account.

B. Encouraging employees to assimilate this philosophy takes time--they must experience your commitment to become believers themselves.

C. All clients should be crucial to you or you shouldn't be doing business with them.

The Right Clients under the Right Terms

Once Bonnie had captured Jack's principal ideas on paper, she turned to the binder he had given her and began to read the section marked "Right Clients/Right Terms." It didn't take her long to digest the five necessary steps. Bonnie's notes outlined the process she read.

III. Right Clients/Right Terms

A. The senior executive and his or her staff are responsible for developing and later articulating the criteria that describe the "right clients" and detail the "right terms."

B. All senior managers should be involved in the following process:

Step 1: Ask the senior managers in attendance to think about and capture the "demographic and psychographic profile" of the "ideal" client.

Step 2: Ask the senior managers in attendance to share their descriptions one criteria at a time, going from person to person, until all the criteria are captured on flip charts and the sheets have been tacked up on the walls of the meeting room.

Step 3: Facilitate a discussion of the criteria. Look for early consensus. Explore conflicting experiences. Encourage debate among the attendees.

Step 4: Identify the "must have" criteria regarding the "right clients" that will not be violated--no matter how good the terms.

Step 5: Conduct the same process regarding the "right terms."

Note: The results should range from "10 to 12" demographic and psychographic criteria. These terms must be clearly articulated by the senior executive and interpreted consistently within the organization.

Just then, Jack hurried in with Bonnie's coffee. "Sorry I took so long," he apologized. "Rosemary can be quite a dragon lady when there are outstanding phone calls to clients. Anyway, what do you think?"

"Just how long does it take to develop the psychographic and demographic criteria?" Bonnie asked.

"Normally about a day," Jack replied. "And it's crucial that all senior managers participate in the process. Otherwise, you end up with second guessing from those who weren't present."

"I've been there before," Bonnie said, ruefully. "And this single process saves fifty percent of all lost business?"

"Bonnie," Jack said "nothing you do will have a more profound or immediate effect on your organization's ability to retain clients."

"How often do you look at the criteria?" Bonnie asked.

"We review it about every six months. As you know, the needs of our organization change and so do those of our clients. We've found by reviewing our criteria with our company's senior executives every six months and then holding our current clients against that screen, we're able to take proactive steps to ensure we're always dealing with the right clients under the right terms."

"And if they don't meet the criteria after the review?" Bonnie asked.

"If the criteria is a 'must have' criteria, we make every attempt to help the client understand our position," Jack replied.

"And if they still don't fit the right clients under the right terms criteria?"

"Then we resign. But that's a drastic measure and it only happens once or twice each year."

Thinking that Jack might just be playing a game of semantics with her, Bonnie faced him squarely and said, "Isn't resigning an account the same as losing one?"

"Not in our opinion. To us, a 'loss' is when you would still like to do business with the client but, in effect, they fire you," Jack said, letting the distinction sink in. "'Resigning' is a proactive management decision that's prudent when the client is no longer the right client under the right terms."

Jack could see Bonnie struggling with this notion, so he expanded on his explanation.

"Look Bonnie," he said, "let's say the key decision-maker changes—which, by the way, is the most common reason for us to review an account—and he or she believes our fees are too high. If we reduce the fees to a level that doesn't provide an adequate return on our investments, in time, we'd resent it and try to find ways to make up the lost profit. From experience, we've realized the things we are forced to do don't always contribute to a relationship built on trust."

Bonnie appeared to be pondering Jack's words. He continued, "and when we accept lower profits that no longer meet our terms, we unknowingly begin to send mixed signals to our people."

"Mixed signals?" Bonnie asked.

"Yep. Our actions would imply that we don't value the account—or them—as highly. Without realizing it—since the account no longer met our terms—the account team would begin to act as if they wouldn't be sorry if we lost it," Jack replied. "Their feelings would come out in the language they used during account reviews."

"And they'd become confused about our organization's dedication to account retention," Bonnie proposed.

"Exactly!" Jack nearly shouted. Somewhat embarrassed by the pitch and intensity of his answer, he grinned sheepishly—but Bonnie was too absorbed in her own thoughts to notice.

"And that's when all the work you've done to build an organizational culture on Attitude and Action begins to fall apart," she mused.

Jack was impressed by Bonnie's quick mind and hoped she was eager to hear more about the controversial aspects of his philosophy.

"Bonnie," Jack said, "what I'm about to say may not sound right, but I can assure you it's true."

Almost imperceptibly, Bonnie leaned forward in her chair.

"We've found it's more profitable to resign an account that

no longer fits our criteria than to continue to do business at the reduced profit levels."

"I'm afraid you're going to have to prove that one to me Jack," Bonnie challenged.

"Glad to," Jack said with an eagerness she hadn't anticipated. "But first, I'll have to ask you a couple of questions. OK?"

"OK," Bonnie responded.

Jack got up, walked to his window, looked at Bonnie, and said, "How much is our reputation worth?"

Puzzled, Bonnie asked, "What do you mean, Jack?"

"If you had to put a dollar value on this division's reputation, what would it be worth?" Jack repeated.

Bonnie could hardly meet Jack's gaze.

"I don't know. I'd have to give it some thought." she replied.

"I'll wait," Jack said, as he turned and looked out the window.

Bonnie knew Jack was serious about waiting. She also knew that he had given this question some thought and that he expected her to do the same.

After a few minutes' reflection, Bonnie said, "I can't put a definite figure on it, but since our top line is a hundred million dollars and the bottom line is six percent of that, I'd say our reputation is worth somewhere between... Oh, Jack, I'd don't know what it's worth!" Bonnie exclaimed in frustration.

"But it's worth millions, isn't it?" Jack asked.

"Probably," Bonnie replied.

"Then why risk ruining a reputation worth millions to save a few thousand dollars in profit from one account?" Jack asked, pausing for effect. He didn't expect a reply.

"What's a referral worth?" he asked almost before Bonnie could mentally shift gears.

"I suppose you'll wait for an answer?" Bonnie said with a grin.

"All the time you need," Jack replied, returning her smile.

"A referral is worth the total of the collective profit during the life of a contract," Bonnie replied almost immediately.

Jack was impressed. It was a much better definition than the one he'd been using. "Great answer," he said. "So, the average profit from one of our accounts is about $200,000 per year, right?"

"Right!" Bonnie responded.

"And currently, an account remains with us an average of twelve years..."

"So that makes a referral worth $2,400,000," Bonnie interjected, finishing Jack's thought.

"And how many referrals does a client, who is in love with your work, provide over the term of his or her career?" Jack asked.

"I don't know," Bonnie said, thinking aloud. "If we followed her throughout her career it might be four or five.

"So that's over $10,000,000 in profit, if my math's right," Jack said.

"Yes, but that's assuming we'd close every lead, and we don't," Bonnie replied. "Still, our closing ratios are about thirty-five percent, so that makes the referrals worth $3,500,000 in profit."

And then it hit her... the company could make $3,500,000 in profit from referrals and maybe millions more in profits because the division had the best reputation in the industry.

"I got it, Jack!" she said, feeling both relieved and inspired.

"I knew you would," Jack affirmed, satisfied with the result of the discussion.

From past experience, however, Jack knew Bonnie would still be struggling with the notion of resigning an account. He walked back to his desk, sat down, and said, "It's not often that we feel compelled to resign an account. But when we do, we 'close' it professionally. We've learned from painful experience that *how you close an account is just as important as how you open one*."

For the first time during their discussion, Jack noticed that Bonnie was taking notes.

He continued, "Often, our clients are forced to take actions they—and we—don't agree with. But they have to take them for business, organizational, or political reasons. We understand that. And they understand our decision when we choose not to do business under those conditions."

"What sets us apart from most of our competitors is that we'll walk away from a marginally profitable situation whereas they'll cut back services in an attempt to maintain profitability. You and I both know how quickly that kind of scenario degenerates."

Past experiences with similar situations flashed through Bonnie's mind.

"But when we walk away, we walk away as professionals," Jack concluded.

"What do you mean?" Bonnie asked.

"Our first step is to sit down with the client and create an exit plan. The plan ensures services to our client will not be disrupted. Then we assist our replacement in every way we can. It includes meeting with the client and our replacement to make sure we provide all relevant information that's not proprietary in nature. Only after our replacement is 'up and running' will we terminate our official relationship."

"Jack, you stressed the word 'official.' What did you mean by that?" Bonnie wondered.

Jack was impressed by Bonnie's listening skills. "One of the things we've learned is that *the end of a contract doesn't mean the end of a relationship*," he replied. "We named our philosophy 'Clients for Life' for a reason. Once you're a client of ours, you're always a client of ours. We'll follow you throughout your career and keep in touch."

"Doesn't that take a lot of effort?" Bonnie asked.

"Yes, it does. But not nearly the effort it takes to learn about and sell a client the first time," Jack responded.

"And, we don't do it just to be nice guys, Bonnie—

although we usually enjoy the relationships we have with our clients. We do it because it provides a constant source of leads and referrals."

"Jack, are you telling me you end up doing business with every one of your past clients sometime in the future?" Bonnie's tone was skeptical.

"No, usually it's about one in three," Jack replied. "But the vast majority remember how we acted when we parted company—so to speak. Even though we're no longer under contract, they're willing to give us positive referrals when potential clients call. As you know, few things are as powerful as a referral from a client who 'wished they could still be doing business with us,' though circumstances prevented it."

"So that's why this division always meets its sales quota with fewer sales people than anyone else," Bonnie observed with a wry smile.

"That's certainly one of 'em," Jack said, putting his finger to his lips in a shushing motion.

"And that explains why it's more profitable to resign an

account that no longer meets the right clients/right terms criteria than to drag on the association and risk ruining the relationship."

"That's right," Jack said. "It's more profitable because we end up with an enhanced reputation, referrals from satisfied clients, and the opportunity to serve our clients again as they pursue their careers. Believe me," Jack continued, "it doesn't make sense to sacrifice what's best for the business in the long term to satisfy some arbitrary short-term financial objective."

"Jack, what else can you tell me about the Clients for Life philosophy?" Bonnie asked.

"Well, I could spend the rest of the day discussing it, but we have a luncheon appointment," Jack answered.

"With whom?" Bonnie asked.

"With the client who just received the bid that's eight percent lower than ours," Jack said with an unexpected twinkle in his eye.

"But I'm not prepared for that. I'm not versed on any of

the issues," Bonnie said anxiously

"The account manager is on top of things, and she'll be able to tell you whatever you need to know. If we leave now, you'll have about an hour together before we meet the client. Not only will Kristin fill you in on the situation, but you'll have time to ask her questions about the Clients for Life philosophy."

"I'm in your hands, Jack," Bonnie said, sensing that resistance was futile.

With that, Jack opened the door and walked to Rosemary's desk. As he checked his messages, Bonnie reviewed the additional notes she'd taken. They read:

> C. The Right Clients/Right Terms criteria should be reviewed every six months.
>
> > 1. A change in key decision-makers is the most common reason to review an account.
>
> D. When a client is no longer willing to do business under the "right terms," resigning an account is a proactive management decision.

1. It's more profitable to resign an account that no longer fits your criteria than to continue to do business at unacceptable profit levels.

E. How you close a contract is as important as how you open one.

1. As soon as you decide to resign an account, devise an exit plan which doesn't divulge proprietary information but keeps the client's operation running.

2. An "official" closing takes place when the firms cease to do business under contract, but unofficial relationships can last a life time.

3. Stay in touch--keeping the personal contacts does take effort, but not as much effort as selling a new client from scratch.

4. Former clients can provide a constant source of leads and referrals.

Keeping What You've Worked So Hard To Get

Kristin met them in the lobby of the building.

"Hi, I'm Kristin," she said as she held out her hand to Bonnie. "I've heard so many great things about you. I'm looking forward to working together."

"Hi," Bonnie replied. "I understand you've done a marvelous job here. Jack speaks very highly of you."

"Oh, Jack speaks highly of all his managers," Kristin said with a laugh and a wink for Jack. "I know you must be eager to update yourself on the situation here; why don't we go to my office and I'll fill you in on the latest?"

"You two go ahead," Jack said as Kristin and Bonnie turned toward the office. "I'd like to wander around and visit with a few people. I'll catch up with you before lunch."

Bonnie was impressed with Kristin's sensitivity to the situation and to her need for information about the contract negotiations on what would soon be her largest account.

As they walked, the two women got to know a little more about one another. Once they were comfortably seated in Kristin's office, Kristin said, "Where would you like me to begin?"

"Well," Bonnie answered, "Jack's told me the competition has underbid us by seven to eight percent. He's acknowledged that that's a lot of money these days, but he doesn't seem worried about the situation. In fact, he told me you had retained the account yesterday. But when I asked him if that meant they'd signed the new contract, he... to be honest, I really don't remember what his answer was. Maybe that's as good a place as any for you to start."

Before Kristin could begin, Bonnie added, "You don't mind if I take a few notes while we talk, do you?"

"Not at all," replied Kristin.

Kristin reached in her top drawer and pulled out the same Attitude and Action paperweight Jack had on his desk. "The cleaning people were in this morning, and I always put this in my desk to be sure nothing happens to it," Kristin said. "If I know Jack, he's already told you about the Clients for Life philosophy and the part Attitude and Action plays in it."

Bonnie smiled. "You know Jack pretty well," she said.

"If anyone in a management services business stands still for more than a few minutes, Jack will be explaining what the Clients for Life process will do for them. He's very proud of what it's done for all of us."

"He should be," Bonnie responded. "You've built the best client retention record in the company."

"I know," Kristin said. "We're all hoping you'll continue to use the Clients for Life philosophy when you assume Jack's responsibilities."

"Based on the performance of this business unit, I'd be crazy not to." Bonnie said. "But help me understand more about it. For instance, why did Jack say you had retained the account when the new contract isn't close to being signed?"

"Oh, that's easy to explain," Kristin responded. "You see, we're convinced client retention isn't an event. It doesn't happen on the day the old contract expires and the new one starts. *Client retention is a daily process.* If we meet our client's expectations every day, then the likelihood of our retaining the contract when the time comes is pretty good."

Bonnie started to ask a question, but Kristin continued.

"In fact, *the worst possible time to begin working on the renewal process is when the contract is due for renewal.*"

"I'm afraid I don't follow you," Bonnie admitted.

"Would you mind if I asked you a few questions, Bonnie?"

Bonnie knew the questions Kristin had in mind were going to cause her to think. After all, Kristin worked for Jack.

"Please do," Bonnie invited.

"Well," Kristin said, "is the contract renewal date a secret?"

"No," Bonnie replied. "It's a matter of record."

"Then it's likely our competitors know when the agreement

is due for renewal. Right?"

"Right."

"And if you were a competitor and knew when the agreement was due to expire, what would you do?" Kristin asked.

"I guess I'd begin working on the client months in advance to determine their needs and to identify any weaknesses on our part."

"Exactly!" Kristin responded with the same sort of enthusiasm Jack had displayed earlier.

"And that's why we can't wait to renew the agreement. If we did, we'd be in no better position than our competitors. We'd have lost the incumbent's advantage," Kristin declared. "Remember," she continued, "it's easy for the competitor to make promises about performance just to get his or her foot in the door. We live or die by the experiences we provide the client every day."

"OK, I see your point," Bonnie said. "But what do you do to renew the contract every day?"

"That's a good question, Bonnie," Kristin said. "For a long time, we couldn't figure out what to do either. But once we had the revelation about the right clients under the right terms — Jack did talk to you about that, didn't he?" Kristin asked.

"Yes, he did." Bonnie confirmed.

"Great. I was ninety-nine percent sure he'd have gone over that idea with you. So, as I was saying, once we understood the power of dealing with the right clients under the right terms, taking the next step became easy. We just protect the client's interests."

"Protect the client's interests? What about this company's interests?" Bonnie said, trying not to sound defensive.

"Oh, Bonnie," Kristin exclaimed, "I'm so glad you asked that question. It's the same question we asked ourselves over and over."

"What answer did you come up with?" Bonnie wondered aloud.

"We realized that provided we've taken the right clients under the right terms, the client's interests and our company's interests are one and the same."

Wham! The brilliance of the approach hit Bonnie like a runaway train. That's why it was so important for the client and terms to be right. Once terms were set, a company could concentrate fully on delivering the service the client contracted for.

"I see..." Bonnie said while the thoughts were still jelling in her mind. "If we protect the client's interests, then we dramatically reduce the likelihood of confrontations with the client."

"That's right," Kristin responded. "And believe me, it's much easier on the account manager to be working with one agenda than with two."

"I know what you mean, Kristin. It hasn't been that long since I was in your chair," Bonnie said empathetically. "I wish the company I worked for then had been aware of the Clients for Life philosophy."

Kristin smiled. She liked the fact that Bonnie had come up

through the ranks and could relate to her situation.

Bonnie continued... "Does that mean you never have a conflict with the client?"

"Not at all," Kristin responded. "It would be naive to think we could run a multi-million dollar program without conflicts. However, when we confront the client, it's because of differences of opinion regarding the right thing to do for the business. But it's never because of how the decision will affect our company's profits."

Kristin continued, "Jack always taught us that when we cared enough about the clients, we'd never be frightened to confront them on any issue."

"And that"—just then, they heard a knock at the door and Jack poked his head in.

"Would you like a little more time alone, or may I join you?" Jack said, flashing that now-familiar smile.

"Come on in," Bonnie invited.

"How's the conversation been?" Jack asked without directing the question to either woman.

"I've learned a lot," Bonnie replied. "Kristin's told me how important it is to renew the contract every day, why the worst time to renew a contract is when it's due for renewal and how we must always protect the client's interests."

"That's great," Jack responded.

"Before we go on," Kristin said, "there's something I need to share with Jack."

Bonnie nodded her consent and Jack asked, "What is it, Kristin?"

"I was talking with the client's controller this morning over coffee. Remember that acquisition they'd been working on? Well, their offer has been accepted. The acquisition will be announced by the end of the week and take place later this month. You know what that means, Jack!"

"I do, I do," Jack said slowly with a hint of concern in his voice.

"What?" Bonnie asked, almost without thinking.

"I'm sorry, Bonnie," Jack said, snapping himself back to

the reality of the moment. "Kristin, why don't you explain the importance of this information to Bonnie?"

"All right," Kristin responded. "It's one of our Lessons Learned℠."

"Lessons Learned?" Bonnie's face revealed her puzzlement.

"Let me explain," Kristin replied. "You see..."

But Jack interrupted. "I'm sorry Kristin. I just noticed the time. Why don't we begin walking to our luncheon appointment and you can explain Lessons Learned to Bonnie on the way?"

As they were getting ready to leave, Bonnie glanced at the additional notes she'd made during her conversation with Kristin. They read:

IV. Keeping what You've Worked So Hard to Get

> A. Client retention isn't an event. It's a daily process.

B. The worst possible time to renew a contract is when it's due for renewal. If you wait until then, you lose the incumbent's advantage.

C. Provided you've taken the right clients under the right terms, your responsibility is to protect the client's interests--which are the same as yours.

1. Protecting the client's interests dramatically reduces the likelihood of client confrontations.

2. When a confrontation does occur, it's focus is on the client's business, not on your firm's profits.

3. You must care enough to confront the client on issues of concern.

Sharing the Lessons Learned

Spring was a great time to be in the South. It was a beautiful, sunny day and just the right temperature to be walking between buildings on their client's corporate campus. As they walked, Kristin and Bonnie engaged in an animated conversation.

"You mean the client acquiring another company has historically meant *our* contract's threatened?" Bonnie said in a tone of mild disbelief.

"Our experience has proven it to us," Kristin replied.

"And you're planning to take the action you described?" Bonnie queried.

"Without question," was Kristin's reply.

"And you're convinced it's warranted?"

"Absolutely," Kristin said firmly.

"I guess I'd better make sure I understand what you've told me about these Lessons Learned," Bonnie said.

Jack was following behind them, but he quickened his step so he'd be a few feet closer as Bonnie began to repeat what Kristin had shared.

"The Lessons Learned are based on the events or changes to the status quo that have consistently threatened the division's contracts over time," Bonnie began.

"That's right," Kristin confirmed.

"And the way you identified them was by bringing all the senior managers in the division together and asking them—what was the question you used?" Bonnie asked Kristin even though she remembered it quite well.

"We asked them to list all the reasons why they had lost business during their careers. The losses had to be based on personal experience. No conjecture or theory was acceptable," Kristin responded.

"And there were seven managers at the meeting?"

"That's right; seven including Jack and me," Kristin replied.

"And the seven of you listed more than forty reasons for losing business."

"That's right, Bonnie. But remember, we all developed our own lists and then took turns sharing the reasons until we had all of them on flip-chart paper taped up in the conference room."

"The charts must have covered all the walls," Bonnie said.

"They did," Kristin agreed, smiling to herself as she remembered what the conference room had looked like.

"And then what did you do?" Bonnie asked.

Kristin didn't mind going over it again. After all, Lessons Learned was a key component of the Clients for Life philosophy.

"Then Jack told us we each could pick three, but only three, of the forty reasons. He emphasized that the three reasons we picked had to come as close as possible to explaining the majority of the losses we'd experienced."

"And," Bonnie said as she finished Kristin's thoughts, "as each of you picked, some of you chose the same reasons. In the end, you had five or six reasons that explained the majority of the losses all of you had experienced in your careers."

"You've got it, Bonnie," Kristin responded with a smile.

"And the client making an acquisition was one of those reasons?"

"Yes, it was an event that had happened to four or five of us," Kristin said. "I know it doesn't sound like it should affect us. But remember, when an acquisition is made, new people join the firm. Sometimes those new people are placed in decision-making positions that affect our operations. And as we all know, when people change, everything has the potential to change."

"Say that again," Bonnie said.

"When an acquisition..."

"No, not that!" Bonnie interrupted, "the part about people changing."

"Oh," Kristin said, somewhat taken back by Bonnie's abruptness. "*When people change, everything has the potential to change*. It was the most common of all of our experiences. When people changed—on the client's side of the desk or on ours—a lot of things happened. Didn't Jack mention that to you?" Kristin said with a questioning look.

"No, Jack didn't," came from behind them in a tone that was partly apologetic and partly playful.

Bonnie turned just as Jack started to speak. "I'm sorry Bonnie, I should have mentioned it earlier. It really is an important part of the Clients for Life philosophy."

"I forgive you, Jack," Bonnie said jokingly. "But don't people move between jobs and companies all the time?"

Jack knew Kristin wouldn't mind if he answered Bonnie's question. "Yes they do," he said, "and it is the single biggest reason for change taking place. After all, we don't do business with a 'corporation' or the name on a building. We do business with the people responsible for those corporations and buildings. And even though the name of the corporation doesn't change and the building doesn't move, when new people assume positions of responsibility, many times it's like dealing with a different company. That's why we educate all of our managers regarding our belief *that when people change* ***everything*** *has the potential to change."*

"Potential to?" Bonnie questioned.

"Yes. The fact that people change doesn't automatically result in changes in our environment, but the potential for change is always there," Jack replied.

"And that's why Kristin is going to take the action she outlined earlier in our conversation. They're designed to protect us in case the new people brought in through the acquisition see things differently," Bonnie observed.

They took a few more steps as Bonnie continued to verbally confirm her thoughts. "…and these new people might see things so differently that they may no longer be the "right clients.'"

"Right!" came from Kristin and Jack almost simultaneously.

Kristin and Jack looked at each other and smiled. It was

becoming clear that they wouldn't have to worry when it was time for them to leave the company. Bonnie was internalizing the Clients for Life philosophy.

They had made their way into the main building where the client was waiting to greet them. As introductions were made, the words "when people change, everything has the potential to change" echoed in Bonnie's brain.

Bonnie reminded herself she'd have to update her notes later. Mentally she went through what she'd learned:

V. Sharing the Lessons Learned

A. Lessons Learned are the handful of reasons that explain the majority of the losses historically incurred.

1. Senior managers are responsible for identifying the lessons learned, communicating these lessons to their employees and sharing the tactics they've used to eliminate these threats.

2. Everyone is responsible for taking the action indicated by the senior managers when one of the threats presents itself.

B. When people change, **everything** has the potential to change.

1. A new client decision-maker might see things so differently as to no longer be the right client under the right terms.

Start-Up: A Crucial Time

As they walked back to Kristin's office, Bonnie couldn't help but think that lunch with the client had provided some keen insights into the Clients for Life philosophy. For instance, even though Jack and Kristin had a wonderful relationship with the client, Bonnie was intrigued by the level of debate—some might call it disagreement—that existed on several issues they'd discussed.

But, she reminded herself, even though there was disagreement, there didn't appear to be any animosity. Their differences were based on individual perceptions of the situation. And the way they took the time to educate each other was refreshing.

Jack had walked the client back to his office. Kristin and Bonnie were alone, walking at a more leisurely pace to Kristin's office.

"I was impressed with the way you handled yourself. You were very poised and confident," Bonnie said.

"Thanks, Bonnie. I owe most of it to Jack. He insists we all go through a selling and negotiating course before we become senior managers. It really helped prepare me for the interactions with the client."

"I'm sorry we're going to be losing you," Bonnie said to Kristin. "When will you be leaving for Hong Kong?"

"Oh, it won't be for three or four months. Maybe longer. It depends on how the negotiations are going on the new contract here," Kristin replied.

"Isn't your husband leaving at the end of the month?" Bonnie asked.

"Yes he is. But as the new managing partner of his firm's Hong Kong office, he's going to be up to his ears in work. Besides he's a big boy; he'll figure out how to get along while I wind up my responsibilities here," Kristin said, to Bonnie's amazement.

"Are you sure?" Bonnie asked.

"Absolutely sure, Bonnie."

As she spoke, Kristin stopped, touched Bonnie's arm gently to stop her, and said, "Bonnie, even though this is your largest account, it's only one of the many you'll be responsible for. But it's the only one I'm responsible for. And the managers in Jack's business unit have pledged to each other that we'll have one hundred percent client retention again this year."

"You know, Bonnie," Kristin continued, "one hundred percent client retention is just a dream for most business units in this company. But we've uncovered the secret to achieving it."

Bonnie listened intently as Kristin spoke softly but confidently. "To have one hundred percent client retention all you have to do is retain one account... the one you're responsible for!" Kristin's passion for her work was unmistakable. "And I have no intention of leaving until I've fulfilled my responsibility to you, my peers, and Jack," she concluded.

Bonnie didn't know what to say. "Thanks," was all that came out of her mouth.

When they reached the office, Kristin stopped by her secretary's desk to pick up messages. Jack was waiting for them inside. Bonnie told Jack of the conversation they'd had on the way back from lunch and said, "Where do you find people like Kristin? She's so dedicated."

Jack felt a great sense of pride. Kristin was one of the first managers he'd hired when he assumed responsibility for the business unit more than a decade ago.

"Remember our philosophy about only doing business with the right clients under the right terms?" Jack asked Bonnie.

"Sure," Bonnie replied.

"That goes for people too," Jack said, just the slightest bit teary-eyed.

Kristin's entrance at that moment allowed Jack to regain his composure. "Jack, did you get the message from A.J.?" she asked.

"No," Jack replied. "I must have missed it. What's up?"

"He wanted to remind you that the Transition meeting℠ with his new clients is this afternoon at three," Kristin reported.

"Thanks, Kristin," Jack said. "I was just thinking that we'd better be going if we're going to make it across town in time."

"What's a Transition meeting?" Bonnie asked.

"I'll fill you in on the way," Jack said.

Jack and Bonnie said their good-byes to Kristin and were off. As they drove to the division's newest account, Bonnie had time to update her notes.

Jack knew he wouldn't have to force the conversation. When Bonnie was ready, she'd take the initiative. After all, in less than half a day, they'd shared insights that had taken him years to discover.

Jack didn't have to wait long.

"So Jack," Bonnie said interrupting Jack's mental performance of the Country song on the car's radio, "what's a Transition meeting?"

"It's a process we insist takes place prior to the start of a new contract," Jack answered. "In fact, we make it part of the terms of every contract we sign."

"OK, but exactly what is it, and why is it so important?" Bonnie probed.

"The meeting assures us that we start the contract according to the client's expectations," Jack replied.

"Don't you use the company's SOP (standard operating procedures)?" Bonnie asked, somewhat confused by Jack's answer.

"We use the parts that are consistent with what the client expects of us. We save the rest until we've established a better relationship. Only then will we begin to educate the client on why we must implement certain procedures and forms to meet those of our requirements that have little direct benefit to the client," Jack continued.

"But doesn't internal auditing and the QA department get all over you for not following company procedures?" Bonnie asked.

Jack could see that Bonnie was struggling with the same issues he had wrestled with years before. He knew he had to explain how and why the Transition meeting was created.

"Bonnie, would you mind if I asked you a couple of questions?"

A small sigh escaped Bonnie before she could catch it. But she smiled because she knew asking questions was how Jack taught. And she was learning a lot. "Not at all," she said.

Jack didn't waste any time. "Have you ever seen a start-up situation in which the manager did everything right? I mean, everything was perfect from a technical standpoint yet the client was disappointed in the manager's performance?"

"Yes, yes I have," Bonnie responded. "In fact, it happened at one of our new accounts in Memphis last month. Our manager did everything we require—a text-book start-up—but the client went ballistic because our manager didn't handle one small item on the client's agenda."

"OK," Jack said. "Now, have you ever witnessed a similar situation where the manager was —oh, let's say—less than perfect technically but the client was pleased with the way things were going?"

"Ever the diplomat, eh, Jack?" Bonnie teased. "Now that I think of it, there was an account of similar size in Rochester. The manager seemed to stumble through the start-up. Our auditors tore him up. But the clients loved the guy and were thrilled with the start-up."

Jack was nodding his head slowly.

"I'm afraid I don't get the connection," Bonnie said as they turned into the driveway of their newest account.

"Just this," Jack said. " How can one client rave about the start-up when the manager fumbles technically while another client becomes irritated with a manager who does everything 'right?'"

Bonnie started to answer, but Jack quickly added, "And don't tell me it's because of the relationship between them. In a start-up situation, there hasn't been time to build a relationship that can withstand the kind of technical screw ups we're talking about."

Bonnie was amazed. That *was* what she had been ready to say.

"Gosh, Jack, what else could it be but the relationship?" Bonnie demanded in a tone tinged with exasperation.

"It's the clients' expectations!" Jack replied with enough enthusiasm to temporarily drown out the radio.

"Each client expected certain things to happen," Jack explained, growing more and more animated. "The manager that 'stumbled,' only stumbled based on the expectations *we* had of him. Apparently, his actions lived up to the expectations the *client* had of him."

Jack's finger was pointing as if he were a member of the Notre Dame cheerleading squad intent on convincing the nation they were number one. "In the case where the manager did everything 'right,'" Jack continued, "he only did what *we* thought was right. Apparently, the client felt that this 'small item' was much more important than our 'textbook' procedures."

"But Jack," Bonnie protested, "unless we have procedures there won't be any continuity or control in our operations."

"Absolutely true," Jack quickly agreed. "But the start-up is a crucial point in the association between firms. Start-up is when the clients are watching to see if we'll live up to the promises made during the sales process."

Bonnie was listening intently as Jack stopped the car in their client's parking lot.

"Many of the promises we make can only be fulfilled during the start-up," Jack continued. "In some cases, we'll get only one chance. We have to do it right the first time. *We must start according to the client's expectations*," he repeated.

"Bonnie," Jack said as he turned off the ignition, "promise me you'll always start the contract according to the client's expectations. Even if it means postponing the implementation of some of our procedures."

The look on Jack's face made it hard to say "no." But Bonnie didn't feel right about promising to ignore company procedures. And Jack knew it. He'd felt the same way—before he learned.

"I'm asking you only to postpone what our company needs until the client's needs have been met," Jack appealed. "I'm not suggesting you deceive the company in any way," he continued, "only that you use your talents to sell management on the need to be patient in implementing some of our required procedures."

"OK," Bonnie replied. "But how will I know when I've lived up to the client's expectations enough to begin implementing our procedures?"

"That's why we're visiting A.J.," Jack said as he opened the door. "Come on, that's A.J. waving to us."

As Bonnie collected her purse and briefcase, she wrote on the corner of her notes...

VI. Start-Up: A Crucial Time

> A. All managers should go through a sales and negotiating course to improve their skills when interacting with clients and with their own managers who influence the start-up process.
>
> B. Always start up according to the client's expectations.

C. The Transition meeting is a process that must take place prior to the start of a new contract.

D. Delay your own firm's SOP (Standard Operating Practices) if it creates a conflict with the client's expectations regarding the start-up.

1. Delaying your SOP does not mean deceiving your own firm; it simply means using your talents to sell management on the need to be patient in implementing some of the required procedures.

The Transition Meeting[SM]

A.J. was the youngest of Jack's managers. He'd been an assistant at one of the firm's larger accounts for two years. In his typical fashion, Jack moved A.J. into the next position just slightly before the young man was ready for it. Jack didn't believe in coasting.

This was A.J.'s first assignment as an account manager. He appreciated Jack's confidence in him and had no intention of letting him down. Even though A.J. was only 26, he'd been the captain of his college baseball team and had leadership qualities Jack himself wished he'd possessed at that age.

"Hey, Jack," A.J. said in his Southern drawl.

"Hey!" Jack responded.

"Ma'am," A.J. replied as he took the hand Bonnie extended.

"Please, it's Bonnie," she said.

"Yes Ma'am," A.J. replied.

Jack always marveled at the combination of A.J.'s deep South upbringing and his Ivy League education. Jack didn't know quite know how to label it, but he hoped A.J. would never change.

"Are we set for the Transition meeting?" Jack asked.

"Yes sir. Our sales rep is waiting in the conference room. Our clients will be joining us at three," A.J. responded.

"Our sales rep? What's she doing here?" Bonnie asked.

"A.J.," Jack said, putting his hand on the young man's shoulder, "why don't you walk Bonnie to the conference room and explain the Transition meeting process on the way? I'll go by the office and escort the clients to the meeting."

A.J. nodded at Jack's suggestion and said "Ma'am," as he moved to the side in order for Bonnie to walk slightly ahead of him.

Jack walked in the opposite direction and glanced back as

Bonnie and A.J. disappeared into the client's education center. Jack was glad he'd been able to orchestrate Bonnie's walk with A.J.. He was confident she'd be impressed with him. And, unless Jack missed his bet, A.J. would be one of the company's leaders someday. He hoped Bonnie would consider being one of his mentors. A.J. could learn a lot from her.

"Besides," Jack thought to himself, "just because retirement is three weeks away doesn't mean I can stop looking out for the best interests of my people."

"So, what's A.J. stand for?" Bonnie asked, trying to make A.J. feel a bit more comfortable.

"Nothing, really, just a nickname my daddy gave me when I was young," A.J. said.

"What's your given name?" Bonnie asked.

"Clarence," A.J. replied but quickly added, "I'd appreciate it if you'd call me A.J., Ma'am."

"Let's make a deal," Bonnie said. "You call me 'Bonnie' and I'll call you 'A.J.', OK?"

"Yes Ma... Bonnie," A.J. stuttered as they both smiled at his struggle.

"Now," Bonnie said, "tell me about the Transition meeting."

"Jack's told you about doing business with the right clients under the right terms hasn't he?" A.J. asked, certain of the answer.

"Yes he has," Bonnie replied. "That and a lot more."

As they walked down the hall toward the conference room, Bonnie continued, "I've learned about the importance of Attitude and Action; that client retention isn't an event but a daily process; that the worst possible time to renew a contract is when it's due for renewal; that it's management's responsibility to resign accounts when necessary because it's more profitable in the long run than running marginally profitable business; that when we resign an account we must have an exit plan that assures the client continuance of service without giving away proprietary information; that keeping in touch with past clients makes sense because it provides referrals and references that lower our marketing costs; that we should always protect the client's interests because it's one and the same with ours and that once we care enough, we'll never be afraid to confront the client on issues of concern."

"Do you believe everything you just said?" A.J. asked.

"I'm not sure yet, A.J. This is my first day with the Clients for Life philosophy," Bonnie replied.

"I believe it. I know it works," A.J. said with such conviction that Bonnie stopped in her tracks.

She looked A.J. in the eye and asked "Really? Does it really work?"

"Yes Ma'am it does. But only if you work at it. There's no free ride. No magic. Just common sense coupled with the Lessons Learned over time," A.J. replied with a maturity much greater than his years.

"The Lessons Learned. I forgot to mention them," Bonnie said.

"They're one of most powerful components of the Clients for Life philosophy," A.J. said. "Think about it, Bonnie," he continued. "I'm 26 years old and yet, because I've been exposed to the Lessons Learned, I have the benefit of more than a hundred years' experience. A lot of the people I went to school with will have to learn those lessons the hard way. And, unfortunately, they'll probably lose clients in the process—clients that could have been saved if they'd only known what to look for and how to respond once the threat became apparent."

A.J. didn't mean to lecture, but he desperately wanted Bonnie to understand how deeply he felt about the Clients for Life philosophy. He was convinced it had advanced him several decades in his quest to become company president.

"I'm sorry Ma'am, I didn't mean to ramble. Daddy always said if you asked me what time it was, I'd tell you how the Swiss felt about their watches."

"Huh?" Bonnie said as his words shook her from her thoughts. She was still thinking about what he'd said. Thinking that if she'd been exposed to the Lessons Learned when she was his age...

"I guess I should tell you about the Transition meeting," A.J. suggested, getting the conversation started again. "I know you realize how crucial it is to start any contract according to the client's expectations."

Bonnie regained her focus. "Yes, I do," she replied. "Exactly how does the Transition meeting help that happen?"

Just then, Bonnie and A. J. entered the conference room where Jan, one of the division's sales representatives, was waiting. Jan stood and introduced herself to Bonnie, and A. J. updated Jan on their previous conversation. After the three colleagues had placed themselves in a seating arrangement that would force their clients to sit between them at the conference table, A. J. continued his explanation to Bonnie.

"The Transition meeting is a simple but powerful tool," A.J. said. "Here's how it works."

"The attendees include everyone in the client's decision-making unit. It also includes our sales representative, the operations manager responsible for implementing the contract, and the business unit manager ultimately responsible for the company's performance. That's why Jan and I are here with Jack."

A.J. paused to allow Bonnie time to ask questions. When she remained silent, he continued with added emphasis, "The Transition meeting also includes any new clients who have assumed positions of responsibility since the contract was signed. That's because..."

Bonnie finished A.J.'s sentence confidently: "because when people change, everything has the potential to change."

A.J. smiled, "That's right," he said. "No matter how recently the decision was made, if a new person becomes involved, we include him or her."

"All right, A.J.," Bonnie said. "I understand who's involved, but what happens once the meeting starts?"

"We begin the meeting by telling the clients how much we want to live up to their expectations of us. And we emphasize that to do so, we must understand what those expectations are," A.J. said, reaching for a stack of yellow cards. "Then we give the clients these 3x5 cards and ask them to write down what they expect of us in the next 30 days, in the next 90 days and in our first year of association."

"Why use 30 days, 90 days and a year as your time frame?" Bonnie asked.

"Actually," A.J. replied, "there's no magic in those numbers. What we're really looking for is an immediate, a short-term and a long-term look at their expectations."

"You ask each client to do this individually?" Bonnie asked to be sure she understood the methodology.

"That's right," A.J. confirmed. " Each client writes down his or her specific expectations for each of those periods. And while they're doing that, we're writing down our expectations of them for the same time frames."

"You mean you tell the clients *you* have expectations of *them*?" Bonnie was incredulous.

"Absolutely!" A.J. replied. "We've made commitments to them based on the situation they described during the sales process. Those commitments are the foundation of the partnership we're intending to build, so it's vital we discuss them openly. For instance, they may have promised we'd have budgets of a certain size. Based on those budgets, we might have promised to do certain things by a certain time. If those budgets change, it's unrealistic to think we can still provide what we promised when the budget was intact. That's the kind of thing we share with them."

"And what happens if they say, 'We're sorry, but the budget is cut and we still expect you to keep your promises?'" Bonnie asked.

"We'd share the reasons why that would be impossible," A.J. replied matter-of-factly.

"And what if they say they'll cancel the contract if you don't agree to their demands?" Bonnie countered.

"Bonnie, if the issue at hand were significant; I mean, if it really affected our ability to perform, we'd thank them for their interest and begin discussing our exit plan," A.J. said with a certainty that made Bonnie squirm in her seat.

"Come on!" Bonnie exclaimed, "No one cancels a contract they've just spent tens of thousands of dollars to obtain."

A.J. looked Bonnie in the eye. "Bonnie," A.J. said, "if things changed to that extent, we'd no longer be dealing with the right client under the right terms. And we are committed to doing business with only those clients. It's a very simple notion."

Bonnie stared at A.J. as Jack's words pounded in her brain... "Our philosophy is simple but powerful. But I won't mislead you; it takes guts to implement. Not that it requires a huge budget. It doesn't. But it does require your time, courage, and commitment."

"Your time, your courage, your commitment. Your time, your courage, your commitment," kept repeating in her head. This morning she'd heard the words, but hadn't understood their meaning. A.J. was living by them.

"How often does the situation come to that?" Bonnie asked A.J.

"One in fifteen or twenty," A.J. replied. "Jack's sent us all to sales and negotiating courses, so it never happens before we exhaust all possibilities of finding a win-win compromise. We can usually find a solution before the negotiations ever degenerate that far."

"But you'd be willing to walk away if it came to that?" Bonnie said, just to make sure she'd heard A.J. correctly.

"Unless you're willing to walk away, you can't negotiate effectively," A.J. confirmed.

Just then, the door opened and Jack walked in with the clients in tow. After making the appropriate introductions and exchanging small talk, A.J. took control and the Transition meeting was under way.

As A.J. conducted the meeting, Bonnie added information about the Transition meeting to her notes. They read...

VII. The Transition Meeting

A. This meeting's attendees include everyone in the client's decision-making unit and the service provider's sales rep, the operations manager responsible for implementing the contract, and the business unit manager ultimately responsible for the company's performance.

B. The Transition meeting also includes any new client decision-makers who have assumed responsibility since the signing of the contract.

C. All clients and service provider participants write down their immediate, short-term, and long-term expectations.

D. These written statements become the basis for open discussion between firms.

E. In the unlikely event that the clients are unwilling to abide by the "right terms"--after exhausting all possible ways of finding a "win-win" solution--the discussion should shift to the creation of an exit plan*.

* Unless you are willing to walk away, you cannot negotiate effectively.

Sales and Operations: A Consistent Message and Mission

It was a little before six as they walked toward the parking lot. Bonnie and Jack had said their good-byes to the clients about an hour ago.

Jack glanced over his shoulder at A.J.'s fifth-floor office. The office lights were bright, and through the blinds he could see the ceiling fan turning slowly. In his mind's eye, Jack saw A.J. and Jan sitting at the table, eating pizza and making the agreed-upon changes to the start-up plan.

Jack knew they'd be burning the midnight oil tonight. But, unlike many of the nights Jack had spent early in his career, A.J. would be adjusting the start-up plan to avoid client problems instead of scrambling to fix them. It was a much easier way to do things.

"So," Bonnie said as they neared the car, "you expected the clients to have different expectations than those Jan said they would have?"

"Absolutely," Jack replied. "One of the things we've learned is that *clients will always have expectations you didn't expect they would have.* But as long as they don't violate the right clients/right terms criteria, we just roll with the punches."

"You don't blame Jan for not knowing what the clients expected at start-up? Isn't that part of her responsibility as the sales representative?" Bonnie asked this question in a way that assured Jack she was not really asking.

He was surprised to hear the hostility in her voice.

"Bonnie," Jack said calmly, "the sales process Jan and her counterparts face is extremely complex. The decision-making unit they deal with is made up of a number of people with different agendas. And their decision criteria change as our competitors educate and we re-educate them during the process."

As Jack walked around to the driver's side, Bonnie stood next to her open door, her eyes glued to him.

"When they see a weakness in our operation," Jack continued, "the competitor's sales people point it out and create the illusion they can easily fix it. They're on the outside looking in, so they create an expectation of higher performance and worry about delivering on it later."

"And," Bonnie countered, "I suppose our sales people never make a promise operations can't live up to just so they can sell the business?"

"Sounds like you've been burned," Jack said, wanting to be certain about the mistrust he thought he heard in her voice.

"Third degree," Bonnie replied without a hint of humor.

"Let's talk about it on the way to your hotel," Jack suggested.

Jack backed the car out of the parking space and headed for the interstate. Bonnie's hotel was one exit east, less than five minutes away. But Jack knew Bonnie wasn't familiar with the city and had no idea how close they were. He decided the drive would take as long as needed to let Bonnie vent her concerns.

"This is the first time I've seen you so upset," Jack said to get the conversation started. "What happened?"

"The details aren't important, Jack. Let's just say we lost a major piece of business in less than a year because a sales person promised operations would do something we couldn't do without giving up all the budgeted profit," Bonnie replied.

"Sounds serious," Jack responded.

"Serious enough that it almost got me fired and cost me my performance bonus," Bonnie said, her voice reflecting her anger at the episode.

"No wonder you're upset," Jack acknowledged.

"The part that upsets me most," Bonnie continued, "was that while we were buried in problems at the account and I was watching a year's worth of work go down the drain, the sales rep was in the Bahamas vacationing—and paying for it with the commission he'd made from selling the account."

"Ouch!" Jack responded, allowing Bonnie to continue to vent her frustration and anger.

"I vowed I'd never let a sales rep do that to me or any of

my people again," Bonnie said with conviction.

Even though she was obviously still upset, the emotion in her voice was beginning to subside.

"You're worried about sales sticking operations in a no-win situation, aren't you?" Jack guessed.

"You've got it Jack!" came Bonnie's quick reply.

"Bonnie," Jack said, "would you believe me if I told you that something similar had happened to me in my career?"

"I guess," Bonnie answered uncertainly.

"Good. Because it has. And it's happened to a lot of operations managers in management service companies where a separate sales department earns commissions based on sales volume," Jack continued.

"Knowing you're a soul mate doesn't make the experience any easier to take," Bonnie replied.

"I know," Jack responded. "But maybe this will."

Giving Bonnie a moment to re-focus on the here-and-now and keeping his eye on the tractor-trailer rig that appeared to be inches from their bumper, Jack said, "That will never happen if you have a Transition meeting prior to the start of the agreement to do business together."

"Why not?" Bonnie replied, groping for the link between her pain and the Transition meeting.

"Because in the Clients for Life philosophy, we don't pay the sales rep's commission until after the operations manager has accepted the assignment. And the operations managers in this district will never accept an assignment until *after* they've had a satisfactory Transition meeting," Jack replied.

"Operations managers *accept* assignments?" Bonnie asked in a puzzled tone.

"Yes. It's sort of our official passing of the baton between sales and operations," Jack replied.

"And operations can turn down an assignment?" Bonnie exclaimed in disbelief.

"Yep," Jack said without hesitation. "If the situation isn't the way the sales person has represented it—that is, if the client has significant expectations that would fundamentally change the nature of contract, the manager can refuse to begin operations."

"Won't the client hold us to the terms in the contract?" Bonnie asked.

"There is no contract until after the Transition meeting," Jack said, emphasizing the point.

Bonnie thought she must have missed something. "What do you mean?" she queried.

"Remember when I said the Transition meeting was part of the contract?" Jack asked.

"Yes. Earlier today when we were on the way to meet A.J.," Bonnie responded.

"Well," Jack continued, "the language in our contract says the Transition meeting will be the venue for final 'negotiations' and contract signing. Naturally, we make sure the language in the contract includes the expectations of both companies as well as all the legal language the lawyers need. If the sales department and clients have been communicating, the Transition meeting is simply a verification of everyone's expectations."

"And if it isn't?" Bonnie asked, quickly grasping the essence of what Jack was saying.

"If there are minor differences, we negotiate them much as we did during the Transition meeting this evening. Then we sign the contract and begin operations," Jack replied.

"And if there are major differences?" Bonnie asked, hoping Jack's answer would be the one she had in mind.

"If there are major differences, the selling process isn't over, is it?" Jack asked rhetorically.

"No it's not!" Bonnie responded. "And that's when the operations manager turns down the assignment and the process reverts back to the sales department. Oh, I love it Jack!" Bonnie said, slapping the dashboard of the Taurus.

Jack just smiled. He figured it was safe to take the next exit and wind their way back to her hotel.

"What does the sales department say about that?" Bonnie wondered, as she realized the implications of what Jack had just told her.

"When? Now or when we first implemented it?" Jack asked.

"Both," Bonnie said quickly.

"Well, now they just accept responsibility for clearing up the misunderstandings," Jack replied.

"What about when the process was first implemented?" Bonnie asked.

"Now that was something," Jack said, thinking back on the political struggle that had taken place.

Bonnie swiveled towards Jack and simply said, "Oh?" while every fiber in her body hoped they suffered!

"Sales was convinced it would be the ruination of the division," Jack began. "They said if we hesitated in providing anything the competitors had promised, the clients might give the business to them."

"Typical sales response," Bonnie thought to herself.

"We pointed out that unless the contract met the right clients/right terms criteria, we didn't care where the business went," Jack continued.

"There it is again!" Bonnie said mentally. "The right clients under the right terms. It permeates everything they do."

"But the fireworks didn't begin until we told them that no commissions would be paid until after a successful Transition meeting had taken place and that we would not, under any circumstances, begin operations without a signed contract." Jack smiled as he savored the debate that had taken place.

"What happened, Jack?" Bonnie asked.

Jack could sense that hearing about the battle would be cathartic for Bonnie, but he knew it wouldn't help her build the bridge she needed with her counterparts in the sales department.

"Clients for Life," Jack declared.

This apparent non-sequitur puzzled Bonnie. "Pardon me?" she said.

"In the end, we all realized it doesn't make sense to start a contract that's doomed to fail just to claim credit against the sales revenue forecast." Jack explained. "For the first time, sales and operations were dedicated—and paid—for the same thing: retaining clients that generate acceptable profits from continuing operations that enhance our company's reputation."

Bonnie stared out the window as she thought about what he had imparted.

"Bonnie, remember I told you I'd explain the fallacy in thinking that growth comes from the next client?" Jack asked.

"Yes, I remember," Bonnie replied.

"In an existing business of any size," Jack began, "your current clients are the key to growth and continued profitability. Any proper financial analysis will prove—all things being equal—that it takes at least three new clients of the same size to deliver the profit of one existing client. Just look at the acquisition and start-up costs associated with new clients and you'll see it's a fact," Jack said with certainty.

"Are you saying we shouldn't worry about getting new clients?" Bonnie objected.

"Not at all," Jack replied. "But, I *am* suggesting that it doesn't make sense to focus resources on getting new clients until you've met the expectations of your existing clients. Otherwise you'll have to find three new ones to generate the same bottom line as you would have from the one client who canceled your contract because you were off chasing new business and failed to perform."

"You know," Bonnie offered, "I've heard that only one organism in all of nature grows for growth's sake."

"And that is?" Jack queried.

"The cancer cell!"

Before Jack could respond, Bonnie added, "Success isn't dependent on growth, but growing profitably. Right?"

"As far as I'm concerned," Jack answered, "top line revenue is meaningless. A gerbil on a wheel has more chance of making progress than a company that gets clients only to lose them because they didn't meet the right clients/right terms criteria."

Raising his finger for emphasis, Jack concluded, "Remember, only a profitable company can continue to provide opportunities for people like Kristin, A.J., and you."

"Just one thing," Bonnie replied as they pulled under the hotel's canopy and Jack put the car into park. "Based on what you told me this morning, everything we talked about only prevents fifty to sixty percent of all potential losses."

"That's right," Jack agreed.

"Well, what about the other forty to fifty percent? What do we have to do to protect it?" Bonnie clearly had every intention of getting an answer.

"Tomorrow's another day, Bonnie," Jack responded.

"I'll pick you up at seven. We'll be attending a training session for our account managers that will provide part of the answer you're looking for."

Bonnie smiled at Jack and said, "Thanks for today, Jack. I learned a lot."

"Me too," Jack replied. "Get a good night's sleep," he called to her as he put the car in drive and slowly pulled away.

Dinner was surprisingly good for a hotel restaurant. After changing into her sweats and calling home to find out what had happened in her family's life, Bonnie stretched out on the bed and reviewed her notes. Under the last one she penciled in her thoughts from the ride to the hotel...

VIII. Sales and Operations: A Consistent Message and Mission

> A. Expect your clients to have expectations you didn't expect they would have--as long as those expectations don't violate the "right clients/right terms" criteria, that's OK.

B. Sales reps can't be expected to foresee all client expectations, but they must be responsible team members.

C. The Transition meeting is the vehicle that keeps sales people from promising more than operations can deliver.

1. Representatives from sales and operations must attend the Transition meeting.

2. At the meeting, operations managers can refuse to accept the assignment.

3. No contract is valid until after the Transition meeting, which is the final stage of negotiations.

4. The contract's language must include the expectations of both companies and must specify that the Transition meeting will make all negotiations final.

5. Operations must not begin work without a signed contract.

6. No commissions should be paid to the sales staff until *after* a successful Transition meeting.

D. The notion that growth comes from your *next* client is a fallacy.

1. In an existing business of any size, to deliver the profit of one existing client takes at least three new clients of the same size.

2. Success depends not upon growth but upon **profitable** growth.

As Bonnie flicked off the light, she smiled and thought "It has been a good day."

If You Leave Client Retention to Chance…

In response to Jack's umpteenth apology, Bonnie said, "Believe me, I understand why you were late. I have two little ones of my own, remember?"

As they drove down the interstate, Jack began to babble again… and he never babbled.

"What are you supposed to do when the baby sitter doesn't show up? The neighbors are gone and relatives are too far away to make a difference. One of the kids has to be at Children's World at eight and the other has a Water Tots class at nine and they're both in the opposite direction of where I need to be. But, you think to yourself, if I hurry and catch a couple of breaks with the traffic I won't be too late. So, you head for the kitchen table to see if they're finished eating breakfast only to find the little one has decided to give herself a Cheerio shampoo. Her clothes are soaked. You grab her and run—run I'm telling you—to the bedroom to change her. But you can't find the suitcase her mother brought with her. And in the background you hear her sister yelling 'pee pee, Grampa, pee pee.' There's no possible way one person..."

"Jack, Jack!" Bonnie called, trying to snap him out of it.

"Huh?" Jack mumbled with a glassy-eyed look.

"I know, Jack, I know," Bonnie said in a soothing voice. "You did the best you could under the circumstances. Everyone's fine. Kim and Melissa are where they're supposed to be and the sitter's car is fixed. We're on our way to the office, and if we're three hours behind schedule, we'll deal with it. Now, tell me what we have planned for the rest of the day."

Bonnie knew the only way to get "Grampa" back in control of himself and the situation was to have him focus on business.

"Well," Jack said as he tried to collect his thoughts, "we won't be able to sit in on the Managing Client Expectations class or the late morning class on Nurturing Professional Relationships. But I've asked two of our best young managers who attended the sessions to join us after they've eaten lunch. That will give you an opportunity to find out what they learned in the sessions."

Bonnie was right; Jack seemed to be able to let go of the morning's fiasco once he started discussing his favorite business topic: Clients for Life.

Jack continued unveiling the remainder of the day's plans.

"We'll be able to catch the end of the session on Technical Delivery before we're due in the President's office."

"The President's office?" said Bonnie, who hadn't realized they'd be seeing him.

"Yes," Jack explained. "He's done a favor for me at one of our accounts and wants to discuss the situation. I'd like you to come along."

"OK," Bonnie responded. "It will be good to see him again."

"Great," Jack replied. "That will leave just enough time to get you to your plane. I can fill you in on the FreshEyes® Review and PostMortem Audits℠ during the drive to the airport."

"Fresh what?" Bonnie asked.

"FreshEyes Review," Jack repeated. "The process is part of the Clients for Life philosophy. It'll make more sense if I explain it after you've heard about Expectations, Relationships, and Technical Delivery," Jack said.

"If you say so, Jack," Bonnie replied. "But it would help if you put today's discussions into context for me."

"I'm sorry, Bonnie. I'd planned to do that first thing this morning. But with all the craziness, it just slipped my mind," Jack apologized. "Let me start with a brief review of yesterday's discussions."

Jack got right to the heart of the matter. "We believe if you leave client retention to chance, chances are you're going to lose clients. Clients for Life is a process for formalizing an organization's approach to client retention. We've learned that you can avoid fifty percent of all losses if you just dedicate yourself to one simple notion: Do business with only the right clients under the right terms."

"It's management's responsibility," Jack continued, "to identify the criteria that describe the right clients and right terms and then to clearly articulate these criteria so they are understood by everyone in the organization."

"To avoid the next thirty percent in potential losses you must educate your people," Jack declared.

"What kind of education, Jack?" Bonnie asked.

"First, is sharing the Lessons Learned with all of the younger managers in our organization," Jack replied. "You learned yesterday about the importance of sharing the historical threats to our business and the tactics that counter them."

"A.J. told me the Lessons Learned gave a 26-year-old the perspective of more than a 100 years' experience," Bonnie confirmed.

"And it does," Jack said with conviction. "The rest of the education process covers managing the client's expectations, developing relationships among all levels of both organizations, and delivering the technical aspects of our service in a way that's consistent with the client's expectations."

"And how do you avoid the final twenty percent of the potential losses?" Bonnie asked.

"Through independent research," Jack responded. "But not the typical 'customer satisfaction' surveys that are so prevalent in most of the services industry. They just don't go far enough to be useful in our environment."

"Why not?" Bonnie wondered.

"Consider the differences between the management services we provide and services provided to a single consumer," Jack said. "You'll never hear the customer satisfaction gurus discuss the complex selling process; the contract that guides the delivery of services; the significant start-up costs; the involvement of multiple levels of management from both organizations; the long-term nature of the association that spans personnel changes; the conflicts in culture and expectations between the companies; the enormous pressures on the account manager; or the staggering impact on profits when a long-term client cancels a contract..."

Bonnie had never thought about just how different it was to provide management services under contract. She'd always assumed that monitoring customer satisfaction was the right thing to do. After all, that's what everyone else did. "What do you do instead?" she asked.

"We conduct two kinds of research. We use the FreshEyes Review with current clients and the PostMortem Audit when we lose a client," Jack responded.

"But I thought our business unit didn't lose clients!" Bonnie's confusion was apparent.

"We don't, Bonnie. But it wasn't always this way. In the beginning, the PostMortem Audit provided us with powerful insights into the mistakes we were making," Jack explained.

"So, the Clients for Life process breaks down into three parts," Bonnie said aloud as she digested what Jack had told her: "Identifying and then doing business with the right clients under the right terms; educating our people regarding the Lessons Learned by the senior management group and then conducting workshops on managing client expectations, developing relationships, and delivering the technical aspects of our service; and finally, using independent research to review our performance at existing accounts and/or to audit why we lost an account when we lose one."

"That's Clients for Life in a nutshell!" Jack said approvingly as Bonnie concluded.

They pulled into the spot in the company parking lot marked "Mr. Jack Henderson." Jack didn't agree with preferred spots. He thought parking should be on a first-come, first-served basis. But after this morning's adventure, he was glad he didn't have far to walk.

"Good morning, Jack, Bonnie," Rosemary said as they entered the office.

"That is a debatable point," Jack responded.

"I think it's a great morning, Rosemary," Bonnie rejoined.

"Here are your messages, Jack. The top three should be returned immediately," Rosemary ordered as Jack walked past her desk.

"OK," Jack said taking off his coat and loosening his tie.

"And, Bonnie," Rosemary added, "there's been a slight change in plans."

"Oh, how's that?" Bonnie asked.

"One of the young managers who was scheduled to meet with you has been asked to attend a working luncheon by his client," Rosemary reported.

"Then I guess that's where he has to be," Bonnie replied.

"He wouldn't have time to attend the late morning session on Nurturing Professional Relationships, so we've rescheduled him for next month. But since his first session is over and there's some time before he has to leave, he wanted to know if you'd still like to meet with him and discuss the Managing Client Expectations workshop," Rosemary explained.

"Well..." Bonnie hesitated, hoping Jack would provide some guidance.

"I think that's a great idea!" came booming out of Jack's office. "Make it so," Jack added.

"He thinks he's on the star ship Enterprise," Rosemary said as they shared a laugh.

"I'm up for it," Bonnie replied.

"Great," Rosemary said. "Why don't you make yourself at home in our small conference room, and I'll ask him to join you?"

As Bonnie waited for Casey to arrive, she took out her notes and added the following.

IX. If you Leave Client Retention to Chance...

A. If you leave client retention to chance, chances are you're going to lose clients. Client retention demands a formal process.

B. To avoid 30% of lost clients, educate your employees in three key areas

1. Managing client expectations.

2. Developing relationships at all levels of both organizations.

3. Delivering the technical aspects of your

service in a way that's consistent with the client's expectations.

C. To avoid 20% of lost clients, use independent research.

1. Customer satisfaction surveys don't work in a management services environment.

2. FreshEyes Reviews monitor current client satisfaction.

3. PostMortem Audits reveal reasons for client defections and help management avoid repeating mistakes.

Managing Client Expectations

"Hi, I'm Casey," said the young man at the door.

Casey was 23 and looked it. He'd been the assistant manager at one of the firm's medium-sized accounts for the past six months. Jack thought he'd make a fine senior manager some day and wanted him to meet Bonnie. The hitch in the morning's schedule provided an excellent opportunity to make it happen.

"Hi," Bonnie replied. "Come on in and have a seat."

"Thanks," Casey said as he settled into a chair opposite her at the conference table.

"I understand you attended this morning's workshop on Understanding and Managing Client Expectations," Bonnie began, trying to make Casey feel at ease.

"Great session," Casey replied. "Now I see why they won't let you take it until you've been exposed to the Lessons Learned."

"Oh?" Bonnie said.

"Yeah, the Lessons Learned gives you the context you need to appreciate the information they communicate in the workshops." Casey said as if he'd been rehearsing for days.

"Just when did you become aware of the Lessons Learned? Bonnie asked.

"I guess the same as everyone else," Casey replied, "as part of my first day's orientation with Jack. I guess you'll be sharing the Lessons Learned with the new hires now?" Casey said.

"You can count on it!" Bonnie responded.

"Good," Casey replied. "We all hoped you'd continue to use what we've learned about client retention."

"I'd be crazy not to," Bonnie said, mentally noting how Casey had used the term "we."

"I'm glad *you* said that," Casey replied and instantly wished he had chosen different words to convey his feelings.

Bonnie grinned and said, "So, tell me a little about what you learned this morning."

"Well," Casey answered, "the class on managing client expectations really opened my eyes."

"How's that?" Bonnie questioned.

"I guess I never realized that clients judge our performance based on their expectations of what will happen, and not on what 'really' happens," Casey said.

He continued, "Clients use a combination of prior personal experiences and the communications provided during the selling process to form an expectation of what our service will be like once we begin operations."

"Are you telling me this from your personal experience or is this what your instructor told you this morning?" Bonnie asked, trying to get a sense of Casey's insight on the subject.

"I don't know," Casey said truthfully. "I think it's a combination of both."

"So why is it important to know that clients use their expectations of what will happen to judge our performance?" Bonnie asked.

"Oh, that's easy," Casey replied. "Because it's critical that we start up according to our client's expectations. Otherwise, we might do things that don't really matter to them. While the things we do may make us feel good, they won't do much to retain the business."

Bonnie probed further: "What else did they tell you about expectations?"

Casey spoke without hesitation. "One thing is that you can create, influence, and manage your client's expectations by using the power of your personal communications."

"Really?" Bonnie said in a non-judgmental tone. "And once you control your client's expectations, what...

"If I said control, I didn't mean to," Casey interrupted. "No one can control a client's expectations."

"Why not?" Bonnie asked.

"There's no way to know about all the prior personal experiences that might affect their expectations. And, beyond that," Casey said with certainty, "you don't know which of your—or your competitor's— communications they'll tune into. There are just too many possibilities to ever think you can control the client's expectations."

"Sounds pretty complicated. With all that going on, how do you know *what* your client expects? " Bonnie asked.

"You know," Casey said, "I had the same question myself when they began to explain this stuff to us."

"Did you get any answers?" Bonnie persisted.

"Yep," Casey replied. "In fact, they told us the secret to understanding our clients' expectations."

"The secret?" Bonnie queried.

"Uh huh," Casey answered. "The secret to understanding what your client expects is to ASK!"

"That's it?"

"Pretty much," Casey confirmed. "We ask in a special way at the beginning of our affiliation with a client. We use a tool called the Transition meeting. It's a..."

"No need to explain, Casey. I attended one that A.J. ran yesterday," Bonnie broke in.

Without hesitating, she continued, "Is start-up the only time you're concerned about the client's expectations?"

"No," Casey replied. "It's a constant process. You see, it's human nature for expectations to change as we have new experiences and are exposed to new communications."

"Human nature?" Bonnie repeated, impressed with Casey's recollection of the session.

"Yes. So it's a good idea to ask periodically how you're living up to your client's expectations. We do it on a quarterly basis," Casey explained.

"Casey, all this theory is great, but what's the practical benefit?" Bonnie waited to see if he'd get flustered.

"Well, the quarterly reviews provide an opportunity to report on our progress against our client's expectations and that reinforces the value we're delivering. These sessions also ensure we remain in touch with what's important to our clients as their competitive environment changes," Casey said calmly. "In fact, our quarterly meeting at the end of the year is often used to get commitments and seek project funding and/or approvals from our clients for the next twelve months."

Bonnie was impressed.

"Mind if I ask you a question?" Casey queried.

"This is contagious!" Bonnie thought to herself as she answered, "Go right ahead."

"You'd like our clients to say they're receiving superior performance from us, wouldn't you?" Casey inquired.

"Naturally," Bonnie replied.

"How would you define 'superior performance'?" Casey asked.

Having no intention of getting worked into a corner by one of her assistant managers, Bonnie replied, "How *should* I define superior performance?"

Casey responded immediately, "Superior performance is performance that exceeds the client's expectations."

"So, to provide superior performance," Bonnie reflected, "the first step is to understand what your client expects."

"That's right," Casey confirmed. "Then you can exceed the expectation by just a little."

"Why not exceed their expectations by a lot and really impress them?" Bonnie shot back.

"Because you're setting yourself up to get zapped by the Expectations Paradox℠," Casey responded.

"The Expectations Paradox? What's that?" Bonnie asked.

Leaning toward her, Casey replied, "The paradox strikes when you provide the client with experiences you can't consistently deliver. Some firms have a habit of doing this at the beginning of a contract. They do special things they wouldn't normally do in an effort to impress the client."

Bonnie listened intently as Casey explained.

"But what they don't realize is that the client uses those experiences to create an expectation of future performance. When a company like ours doesn't provide the same level of performance once normal operations get underway, the client becomes disappointed. In effect, we'd fail to live up to the expectation *we* established," Casey concluded.

"So what do you do to avoid being trapped by the Expectations Paradox?" Bonnie asked.

"Three things," Casey replied.

"Understand your client's expectations by asking what they are."

"Provide superior performance by exceeding their expectations, but by just a little."

"And do steps 1 and 2 over and over until you can no longer beat your past performance."

"What happens then?" Bonnie asked.

"That's when you use the power of your personal communications. You begin to prepare them to accept that *maintaining* a given level of performance is, in fact, superior performance," Casey replied.

"Are you saying the client shouldn't expect any future increases in performance?" Bonnie asked.

"No," Casey explained, "we never stop searching for little incremental improvements or fine tuning what we've done. But, once we deliver our best, we manage the client's expectations to a maintenance mind set."

"And they buy this?" Bonnie said in a skeptical voice.

"Sure, if three things happen: they trust you, it's the truth and the competition can't do any better," Casey responded.

"What if..."

"Sorry for the interruption," Rosemary said as she poked her head in the door, "but if Casey's going to make his luncheon meeting, he needs to get on his way."

"Yo," Casey said looking at his wrist watch, "I gotta get a move on. I hope I helped you get a sense of what they taught us this morning."

"You did," Bonnie said. "Drive carefully. I'll see you in a couple of weeks when I visit your account with Jack."

"Great! See you then," Casey said as he darted out the door and jogged down the hall.

"Youth is wasted on the young," Rosemary observed as she watched Casey bound down the stairs. "Are you ready to see Maria?"

"Just give me a minute or two," Bonnie replied. "I'd like to make some notes."

"Sure, just give me the high sign when you're ready," Rosemary responded.

"OK," Bonnie said as she pulled her notes from her brief case.

To the notes she'd already taken, Bonnie added...

X. Managing Client Expectations

A. The next thirty percent of potential losses can be saved by educating your managers. The first piece of information they need is how to understand and manage their clients' expectations.

B. Expectations are formed from prior personal experiences and all forms of communication—particularly those used during the selling process.

1. To judge our performance, clients use their expectations of what will happen and not what "really" happens.

2. Client expectations are constantly changing as clients have new experiences and are exposed to new communications.

3. By using the power of personal communications, it's possible to create, influence and manage client expectations, but not to control them.

4. The secret to understanding client expectations is to ASK.

a. Ask your clients about their expectations on a quarterly basis to stay in touch with client needs, reinforce your value to the client and obtain funds or approvals forfuture projects.

C. When dealing with clients, deliver superior performance, but beware of the Expectations Paradox.

1. Clients for Life defines superior performance as performance that exceeds the client's expectations.

2. Exceed the expectation, but by just a little or suffer the consequences of the Expectations Paradox.

3. The Expectations Paradox strikes when you provide the client with experiences that you can not deliver consistently.

4. Clients will accept the service provider's limits under three conditions:

a. The client trusts you.
b. The limits are real.
c. The competition can't do better.

Nurturing Professional Relationships

Maria was twenty-two. She'd recently graduated with honors and had been hired as an assistant manager only last month. Jack was impressed with her approach to problem solving and blown away by her near photographic memory. He thought she had a great future with the firm. With Bonnie's help, she'd rise through the ranks quickly.

"Come on in," Bonnie said cheerfully as Maria knocked on the open door.

"Hello," Maria said.

"I hate to have a table between me and the person I'm talking to. Would you mind sitting over here?" Bonnie asked, motioning to the chair beside her.

"Not at all," Maria replied.

"I understand you just finished the session on Nurturing Professional Relationships," Bonnie began.

"Yes, just a few minutes ago," Maria confirmed.

"So, what did you learn?" As Bonnie asked, she noticed that time was passing more quickly than she'd realized.

"Not much," Maria replied.

"What?" Maria's answer had caught Bonnie off guard.

"Oh, pardon me," Maria apologized. "I didn't mean that the way it sounded. There just seems to be little difference between managing professional relationships and managing personal relationships."

"How's that?" Bonnie asked.

"Well, my Mom and Dad taught me a long time ago that the most important things in any relationship were trust and respect. That if you shared those things, most of what happened could be worked out," Maria said. "Wouldn't you agree, Bonnie?"

"Yes, I would" Bonnie responded, noticing how naturally Maria used her selling skills to gain agreement.

"Essentially, that's what they told us this morning," Maria continued. "What I found fascinating were the suggestions on how to build trust in a business environment that's governed by a contract."

"What did they suggest?" Bonnie asked.

"They said trust was built by consistently implementing three specific behaviors," Maria said, emphasizing "consistently," just as the instructor had.

"Which are?" Bonnie prompted.

"Candor, competence, and concern," Maria responded.

"How do you demonstrate these traits?" Bonnie asked.

"Candor is telling the client what they need to know even though it may not be what they'd like to hear," Maria began. "Competence is consistently delivering superior performance without becoming entangled in the Expectations Paradox. And concern is treating the client's business, and decisions that affect it, as if the business were your own."

"Very good," Bonnie said in acknowledgment of Maria's explanation. "Do you believe what you've just said?"

"I think so. It's pretty consistent with how I've behaved growing up. But I must admit, sometimes being candid results in a confrontation. And I'd rather not confront people," Maria said, sharing her vulnerabilities.

"I felt the same way, Maria," Bonnie responded. "It's a natural reaction. Don't worry, though, we'll expose you to education on how to properly and comfortably confront someone."

"Great!" Maria replied.

"What did you learn about gaining the respect of others?" Bonnie queried.

"That I'd have to stand up for what was right," Maria replied.

"That can be difficult to do sometimes," Bonnie observed.

"I know. And I understand that it won't be without consequences. But, as the Aaron Tippen song says, You've got to stand for something, or you'll fall for anything," Maria declared with confidence.

"Learn anything else?" Bonnie asked, impressed by Maria and her answers so far.

"Yes, the Web of Influence® was eye-opening!" Maria exclaimed.

"What's the Web of Influence? Bonnie asked.

"It's our way of assuring the retention of the business will never depend on a relationship with one person—no matter how high in the client's organization," Maria replied.

"How does it work?" Bonnie pursued.

"Well, every person in our organization is required to have a business relationship with the people who can hire us, fire us or significantly influence that decision. And—this is the web part—" Maria said with a bit of intrigue in her voice, "we also have to have a business relationship with the person one level up and one level down from our direct counterpart in the client's organization."

Although Bonnie nodded in agreement, she looked a bit puzzled.

"Let me show it to you," Maria said. "It's much easier to understand once you see it on paper."

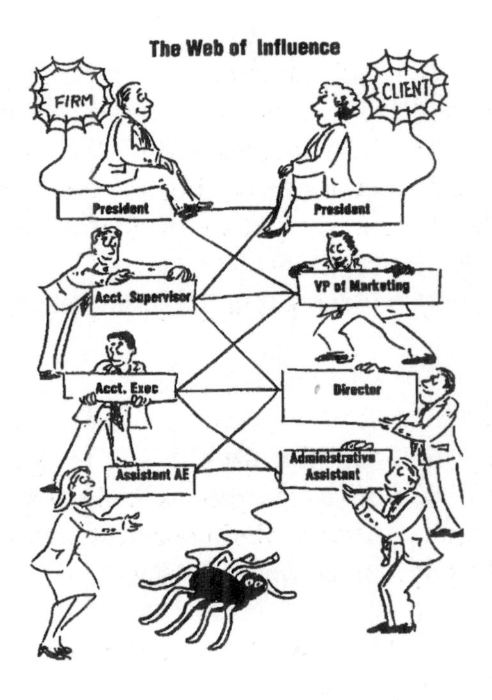

Bonnie looked over her shoulder as Maria referred to the material on the Web of Influence from the workshop she had just completed.

"Maria, you said each level was responsible for developing a 'business relationship.' Just what do you mean?" Bonnie asked.

"Oh, I'm sorry," Maria said, embarrassed that her explanation had been incomplete. "I meant that the three people I'm responsible for connecting with must know who I am, must trust and respect me, and must be willing to meet with me provided I give them a valid business reason for the meeting."

"I understand now," Bonnie replied. 'Anything else get your attention this morning?"

"Yes! Building a database of information about each of our clients. That's a great idea," Maria replied. "They gave us a form with the information the company would like to have on each of our clients." At this, Maria opened her workshop binder to the page containing the form.

"How do you feel about keeping this kind of information on your clients?" Bonnie asked.

"I don't have a problem with it. Why would clients mind if you kept information like home town; college attended and major; marital status; anniversary date; spouse's name; home address and phone number; children's names and ages; hobbies; favorite restaurants; clubs and associations; political affiliation etcetera?"

"You're right," Bonnie interrupted, "the vast majority of them don't."

"It's like Harvey Mackay once said, "People don't care how much you know about them once they know how much you care about them," Maria responded.

"I couldn't agree more!" came Bonnie's quick affirmation.

"I imagine Jack's database is going to be extremely helpful as you assume his responsibilities," Maria observed.

"I honestly don't know what I'd do without it. Ten years of insights all laid out for me. It amazes me that we once relied on account managers to keep this information in their heads," Bonnie replied.

"Yeah," Maria said. "And when they left the company, the information left with them. But with computers and the internet, there's no excuse for not keeping this information so the company always owns it and has access to it when it's needed."

"Maria, I've enjoyed our conversation, and I'm looking forward to getting to know you better," Bonnie said as she noticed it was almost time to meet Jack. "Is there anything else you think I should know about this morning's session on relationships?"

"Just that trust takes a long time to build, but it can be lost in a split second," Maria replied.

"Don't ever forget that," Bonnie implored as she stood to shake Maria's hand.

"I won't," Maria promised as she walked toward the door.

"I'll see you in a couple of weeks when Jack and I visit your account," Bonnie said in closing.

"I'm looking forward to showing you our account. You'll be proud," Maria replied.

"I'm sure I will," Bonnie responded. "Will you do me a favor and tell Rosemary I'm on my way?"

With a nod and a last smile, Maria turned and walked down the hall.

Bonnie went back into the conference room, took out her notes, and added...

XI. Nurturing Professional Relationships

A. Like personal relationships, professional relationships flourish when they're based on trust and respect.

1. Trust is created by consistently demonstrating candor, competency, and concern.

2. Trust takes a long time to build but a split second to lose.

3. Respect is gained when you take a stand on the things people know are right.

B. Always weave and maintain a Web of Influence.

1. Never let the contract depend on one business* relationship, no matter how high

in the client's organization.

* A business relationships means that your client knows you, trusts and respects you and will meet with you--provided you have a valid business reason for meeting.

2. Every one of our managers must be tied to three in the client's organization.

3. Our web of influence must include the people who can hire us, fire us, or significantly influence that decision.

C. Create a database of information on each client.

1. This information should include the client's home town, college attended, marital status, anniversary date, spouse's name, home address and phone number, children's names and ages, hobbies, favorite restaurants, clubs and associations, etc.

2. A database like this is crucial to maintaining client relationships as people transfer within the company or leave to pursue their own careers.

Solving Problems and Delivering Innovation

"I'm sorry I'm a few minutes late, Jack; can we still visit the Technical Delivery workshop?" Bonnie blurted as she hurried into Jack's office.

"Sure, we'll be in time to catch the recap," Jack responded. "By the way, how did your conversations go with Casey and Maria?"

"Great! I was impressed with both of them. They did you proud, Jack," Bonnie replied.

"I knew they would," Jack said. "Being with them makes me wish I were starting all over again."

Bonnie knew Jack's statement didn't require comment.

"Come on, let's walk over to the large conference room and see how the workshop is going," Jack said, motioning to Bonnie.

They opened the door at the rear of the conference room and slid into the back row of chairs as the instructor brought the workshop to a close. The company tenure of the eight assistant managers in attendance varied from two to six months.

"So," the instructor asked, "who can tell me what clients expect from a technical standpoint?"

Allison, who was the newest member of the management team responsible for the district's second-largest account, spoke up. "Two things: they expect us to solve their problems and bring innovation to their business."

"Absolutely," the instructor confirmed. "And what's the key to solving the client's problems?"

"Having agreement on what the problems are and understanding the priorities the client assigns to getting them fixed," Allison responded.

"Exactly," the instructor responded.

"Now, someone else tell me what an innovation is," he asked the class.

"An innovation is something clients are not yet doing for themselves," came Tracy's reply.

"OK, Tracy," the instructor retorted, "does the innovation have to be something brand-new to our firm?"

"On the contrary," Tracy replied, "many of the things clients consider innovations are second nature to us. In fact, we must guard against becoming apathetic about our systems and capabilities. We take things for granted because they're part of our expertise when they're really special to people who have not seen or used them before. And when we use these innovations to solve problems for the client, we must remind them of the service we provided by documenting our successes."

"Why document our successes?" the instructor asked.

"Because our failures will document themselves. *We* are responsible for making sure the client's file regarding our firm accurately reflects our overall contribution to their business," Tracy replied with confidence.

"To what purpose?" the instructor prodded.

"To ensure that if and when a client changes, the paper trail his or her successor inherits will help us make a good first impression," Tracy shot back.

"Couldn't have said it better," the instructor affirmed with a nod of approval. "Are there any questions about what we've discussed this afternoon?"

The room was quiet. After a few moments he said, "It looks like we're finished. If you'll please fill out the comment sheets and turn them in, I'll conclude by saying thank you for your attention. I'm looking forward to seeing each of you in another session."

As the class members completed their evaluation forms, Bonnie took out her notes and added...

XII. Solving Problems and Delivering Innovation

A. From a technical standpoint, clients expect a services provider to solve their problems and bring innovation to their business.

1. The key to solving a client's problems is agreement on what the problems are and understanding the priorities the client assigns to getting them fixed.

2. Innovation is something clients are not yet doing for themselves.

3. Innovation need not be a skill newly acquired by the provider to be a revelation to the client.

B. Document your successes; your failures will document themselves.

1. Documentation of success will leave a paper trail beneficial to your organization in times of change.

"We got here just in time, Jack," Bonnie said as the last of the class left the room.

"Speaking of being just in time," Jack replied, "we'd better get going if we don't want to be late for our appointment with the President." Jack took Bonnie by the arm and headed for the door.

As they walked down the hall, Jack said, "You know, it's getting hot outside. I think we ought to take the car. Wait right here. I'll get my keys and be back in a minute."

While Jack walked back to his office, Bonnie reviewed her notes and began to appreciate why education in these areas was the key to preventing thirty percent of potential lost business.

Before she realized it, Jack had returned. She didn't hesitate to ask a question that had occurred to her while he was gone.

"Jack," Bonnie said "which is the most important part of the education process? Is it educating our people to manage the client's expectations? Or is it developing and nurturing professional relationships? Or is administering the technical delivery of our services the most important?"

"Which do you think it is?" came Jack's response.

"If I had to choose, I'd say it's the development of the relationship," Bonnie replied. "But I'm not really sure."

"A good relationship will buy you time to fix a technical screw-up," Jack confirmed, "but having a good relationship alone isn't enough to survive."

"Then what's the answer?" Bonnie persisted.

As Jack opened his door, he said, "Get out your notes."

Once he was comfortably seated behind the wheel, Jack took Bonnie's notes and at the bottom of the page drew a child's teeter totter.

"The answer to your question is that you must educate your people to manage *all three* of these areas. Having one or two simply won't get the job done," Jack said in the same passionate tone Bonnie had heard before.

"It's like a child's see-saw," Jack explained pointing to the drawing he'd made. "Understanding the client's expectations makes everything possible. But we deliver on the client's expectations by managing the relationships and technical aspects of our service.

Bonnie nodded her understanding.

"At times, the relationship will require the most effort. At other times, the technical aspects will have our attention. And don't forget," Jack added, "that how we live up to the client's expectations of our technical expertise will impact the relationship and visa versa."

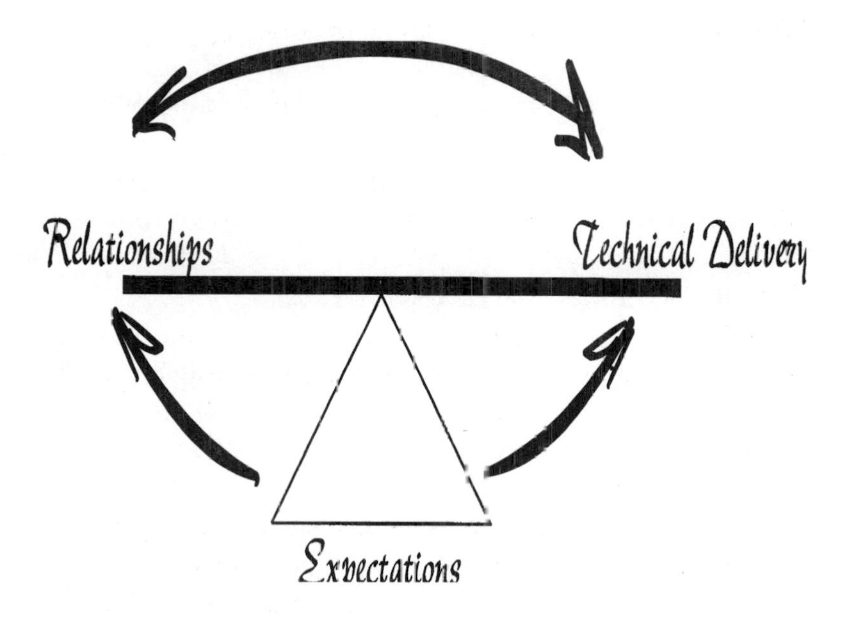

Bonnie watched as Jack drew arrows that linked the three areas.

"Managing all three, all the time. That's what it takes," Jack declared as he backed the car out of the parking space and headed for the President's office.

The FreshEyes® Review and PostMortem Audit[SM]

"Hi, Kathy," Jack called out as he entered the reception area of the President's office.

"Hi, short timer," the President's secretary responded.

"Is Bill ready for us?" Jack asked.

"Go right in. He's eager to see both of you," Kathy replied.

As Bonnie and Jack entered the office, Bill stood and walked toward them. Holding out his hand, he said, "Bonnie, it's so good to see you again. How's the orientation going?"

"I couldn't ask for more. Jack's taking good care of me," Bonnie replied with a smile.

"I wouldn't expect anything less from this guy," Bill acknowledged, nodding his head in Jack's direction.

"And how are you doing, my friend?" Bill asked with genuine concern.

"OK, I guess. It just doesn't seem like it's been twenty-seven years since you and I joined the company as assistant managers," Jack replied with a shake of his head.

"I know what you mean," Bill said. "In another two years, I'll be right behind you. And then, Jackie, we can chase the little white ball and cast for bigmouth any time we want."

Bill and Jack looked at each other and smiled. They'd been friends a long time. They both knew they would have stayed with the company forever if it were possible. Both of them loved the satisfaction their work provided.

"Let's sit down over here," Bill suggested, motioning to the sofa and chairs. "Can I get either of you something to drink? Coffee, soft drink, iced tea?"

"Nothing for me," Bonnie responded.

"I think I'll have a little sweet tea," Jack replied.

As Bill asked Kathy to bring them two glasses of tea, Jack took the results of the FreshEyes Review out of his brief case.

During the drive to Bill's office, Jack had explained to Bonnie that to prevent the final twenty percent of all potential losses, they needed an independent assessment of their performance at every account. The FreshEyes Review was the company's process for accomplishing this task.

The "FreshEyes," as it was known within the company, was conducted annually at all key accounts or when a significant event or change occurred. The review was conducted by an independent consulting firm.

Bonnie questioned the need to use an outsider and shared her concerns about what the clients might think. Jack explained that in 99.9% of the cases in which a FreshEyes Review was conducted, the client applauded their efforts. Besides, he had learned years before that there were too many political agendas for an insider to conduct the review and keep the information unbiased.

Jack had requested a FreshEyes Review on an account where the client's president had just hired a key vice president. Jack and Bonnie were going to see Bill to discuss the results of the review and to hear what his sources could add to the information the FreshEyes Review had uncovered.

"I see you're ready to talk business," Bill said as he joined them.

"I'm a little concerned," Jack responded. "What did your sources have to say?"

"They verified the concerns expressed in the FreshEyes," Bill responded. "The new VP has had three different positions within the past seven years. In each one, she's brought in our competitor at the first opportunity she's had. It appears she has a close personal relationship with the president of the firm."

"Just what we need," Jack sighed.

From reading the report, Bonnie knew there were no problems on either the technical or relationship side of the business. Each person interviewed spoke highly of the company and the job the account team was doing. Expectations were met or exceeded on every key project.

Kathy brought in the tea as Bonnie said, "But the new VP has never inherited one of our operations before. Right?"

"That's right. And she's never come in at this level before. Until now, she's come in at the Department Manager level and has been responsible for day-to-day operations," Jack replied.

"So, what action are you planning to take, Jack?" Bill asked.

Bonnie could sense that even though Bill and Jack were old friends, when it came to retaining accounts, Bill was all business.

"First, let me say to both of you, that I have no intention of losing this contract. We've worked too hard and are providing too much tangible value to our client," Jack responded with conviction.

Attitude and Action flashed through Bonnie's mind.

"How will we minimize this threat?" Bill pursued.

"Our first step is to visit with the clients in our Web of Influence," Jack said quickly, having thought about his action steps beforehand. "Bill, I'd like you to call the president of the company. You haven't played eighteen with him in a while have you?"

"No, we haven't. And, as I remember, it's my turn to host the outing," Bill responded.

"Great!" Jack replied. "I know I don't have to coach you on what to do."

"You've been coaching me half your life, Jack," Bill said with a grin.

"It's nice to see you're finally responding to all that effort," Jack shot back. They both laughed.

"I'll follow up with the president after you and he have met," Jack continued.

"Bonnie," Jack said, "you and I will visit with our liaison when you're back in town next week. He reports directly to the new VP."

"OK," Bonnie replied. "And I can have our team arrange meetings to introduce me to all of their counterparts. We can use the meetings to reinforce our value and the positive changes that have occurred since we've become involved."

"Great idea!" Jack responded. "And we'll both introduce ourselves to the new VP."

Bonnie agreed, and Jack continued "During the meeting, I'll suggest to the new VP that we do a Transition Lite[SM] presentation. Since both she and Bonnie are new, it would be an excellent time to review our involvement."

"Transition Lite?" Bill asked.

"Sorry, Bill." Jack responded. "It's the name I've given to a process you and I have used many times. It's the process where we review the condition the account was in when we accepted management responsibility; where we are now; and where we plan to take it."

"A Transition meeting—only shorter and with one person." Bill said, nodding.

"Right. Calling it the 'Transition Lite' just makes it easier to remember and teach to our young people," Jack explained. "At the end of the presentation, we'll ask the new VP to share her vision of the future. Our account team will then create the action steps necessary to make that vision a reality."

"Do you think the steps you've outlined will be enough to retain the account?" Bill asked.

"Enough until we meet with the new VP and find out what her plans are," Jack replied.

"Don't worry Bill," Bonnie interjected, "you have my word that we'll do everything in our power to keep this account. I've no intention of beginning this assignment by losing a contract."

"Let me know how I can support you," Bill replied.

"I will," came Bonnie's quick response.

"Before we move on to something I'd like to discuss with Jack, I'd like to know how we're doing at your largest account. I understand we've been underbid by eight percent?" Bill said, looking at both of them.

"Let me answer that one," Jack replied, knowing he hadn't kept Bonnie up to date on what was happening. "Based on Kristin's team's analysis of the situation, we're convinced the competition's bid isn't an 'apples to apples' comparison. We've discussed the difference with the client and we're convinced we're less than two percent apart."

"How does the client feel now that we've explained the facts?" Bill asked.

"He's upset! Whatever advantage our competitor had hoped to establish by putting in such a low number has just gone down the drain," Jack responded.

"You reap what you sow," Bill replied.

"What about the two percent difference?" Bonnie asked.

"We'll sell around it," Jack said. "If we can't demonstrate our win-win approach is worth two percent, we deserve to lose this account."

Now that Bill felt comfortable with the business situation, he turned to more personal matters. "What are you going to do after you retire, Jack?" he asked.

"Travel a bit—I've always wanted to see the outback in Australia. Putter around the house. Play some golf with the guys. Visit the grandchildren. That kind of stuff. Why?" Jack replied, a bit confused because Bill knew very well what Jack's plans were.

"Would you consider doing some PostMortem Audits for me in another division?" Bill asked.

"PostMortems?" Jack repeated.

"I'm afraid so," Bill confirmed. "Clients for Life hasn't been implemented yet in several of the acquisitions we've made during the past year. I really need your help. We've lost some accounts and the closing reports I'm getting are a bunch of BS," he explained. "They point the finger in every direction but where it should be pointed."

Jack couldn't help but think back to the time when he and Bill were formulating many of the processes that had become Clients for Life. The PostMortem Audit was one of the earliest and most valuable. Using an independent third party to interview clients who had canceled contracts, the reports provided unbiased and undistorted information on the mistakes the company was making. Mistakes that could be corrected-- but only if they were acknowledged.

"You mean you want me to be the independent? The person who asks where we failed to live up to the client's expectations, manage the relationships, and provide the technical aspects of our service?" Jack asked.

"You're it," Bill chuckled.

"Can I have some time to think about it?"

"Sure, but I need your decision by the end of the month. You know how critical it is to follow up within a couple of months of the cancellation date," Bill reminded Jack.

"I know," Jack replied. "I'll let you know by then."

Bill rose, signaling Jack and Bonnie that the meeting had ended. "Where are you two off to now?" he asked.

"My plane leaves at five-thirty, so we'll be heading for the airport," Bonnie answered.

"Have a safe flight home," Bill said. "And learn as much as you can from this guy during the next few weeks. He's one of the best that's ever been."

"I will," Bonnie replied fervently, "and thanks for the vote of confidence. I won't let you down."

"Don't thank me—I think you'll make a great senior manager—but Jack is the one who insisted that you replace him," Bill revealed, as Jack gave him a 'why'd you have to tell her that?' look.

"Really?" Bonnie could not hide her surprise and delight.

"Yep, said he wouldn't retire unless you were selected as his replacement," Bill continued.

"No kidding?" Bonnie marveled as she and Jack walked toward the door.

"We'd better go," Jack advised, "or her head will get so big it won't fit through the door of the airplane."

"See ya, partner," Bill said as they left.

"Thanks, Bill," Jack replied as he shook Bill's hand. "I'll be in touch about doing the PostMortems."

Since it was growing late, Jack dashed off to get the car, and Bonnie made these notes while she waited for him to return.

XIII. The FreshEyes Review and the PostMortem Audit

A. Both of these processes must be done by unbiased, third-party individuals or organizations. Action must be taken based on the information each of the processes provides.

B. The FreshEyes Review should be conducted annually at all key accounts and/or when a significant event or change occurs for a client.

1. The FreshEyes Review asks these questions:

a. How are we living up to the client's expectations?

b. How good are the relationships between the people representing the organizations?

c. How effective is the delivery of our technical services. Are we solving the client's problems and delivery value?

C. A PostMortem Audit should be conducted within two months of the time the contract is canceled.

1. PostMortem Audits ask these questions:

a. Where did we fail to live up to the client'sexpectations?

b. Where did our Web of Influence break down?

c. Where did the technical aspects of our service fall short?

D. Mistakes can be corrected only after they've been acknowledged.

E. To reinforce your value to a client, engage in the Transition Lite: Review with the client the condition of the business when you first assumed responsibility for the account, its condition now, and the clients expectations for the future.

Client Retention demands a Formal Process

"So I was your pick?" Bonnie asked as they drove through the city.

"Don't let it go to your head," Jack retorted with that smile of his.

"Why me?" Bonnie persisted, hoping Jack wouldn't take the question lightly.

"Honestly?"

"Honestly!"

"Well, everyone that was considered had great qualifications," Jack began. "From a technical standpoint it was a draw. Where you stood out was in your regard for the people in our organization. You didn't see them as employees but as your partners. That attitude is critical in a lot of areas, but it's vital to the Clients for Life philosophy. And continuing to use Clients for Life is critical to your future success."

As they eased into the interstate traffic, Jack further shared his response to her question.

"Bonnie," Jack explained, "you were the only one who believed we could continue to have 100 percent client retention. All the rest looked at our record and wondered aloud when 'something' would happen that would cause the loss of an account."

"Really?" Bonnie said, not knowing what else to say.

"Yes. And the worst—the worst—thing that can ever happen to an organization is to have the leadership begin to doubt it can accomplish its objectives," Jack asserted with conviction.

"So, the success of Clients for Life begins with me, is that what you're saying, Jack?"

"What I'm saying is that the moment you doubt 100 percent client retention is possible, the attitude of this organization changes," Jack responded.

"And it all begins with attitude, doesn't it Jack?" Bonnie said as she reflected on their first conversation the day before.

"Attitude..." Jack began

"and Action!" they finished together.

"Jack," Bonnie said seriously, "don't worry. I'll keep the faith."

"You wouldn't be here if I didn't think you'd make me proud," Jack replied without taking his eyes from the road.

Bonnie smiled. She knew Jack had made the right choice.

The rest of the ride to the airport was filled with the kind of casual conversation people share when they're first getting to know each other. Kids, hobbies, passions. Jack told Bonnie about his penchant for bass fishing, and Bonnie shared stories about her daughters—the pride of her life.

The 45 minute ride was over before Bonnie realized it. As they unloaded the trunk, Jack confirmed where he'd meet her next week to continue the transition and helped her to the curbside check-in. They shook hands and before Bonnie knew it she was watching him drive off.

Bonnie made her way to the gate, took a moment to check voice mail, boarded the aircraft, and collapsed into seat 10-C.

Once the jet had leveled off, Bonnie reached for her notebook. She wanted to sum up her experiences while they were still fresh in her mind. Over a glass of white wine, she reviewed her notes and then distilled what she'd learned into what she called the ten Commandments of Client Retention

She wrote…

1. Client retention begins with the right clients under the right terms.

2. Start the contract according to the client's expectations.

3. Expect your client to have expectations you didn't think they would have.

4. Always protect your client's interests.

5. Client retention is not an event, it is a daily process.

6. When people change, everything has the potential to change.

7. Keep track of past clients throughout their careers.

8. The worst time to renew a contract is when it is due for renewal.

9. The end of a contract doesn't have to mean the end of a relationship.

10. How you close a contract is just as important as how you start one.

Happy with her efforts, she decided to represent the Clients for Life process in a diagram anyone could understand.

The Clients for Life®
Client Retention Process

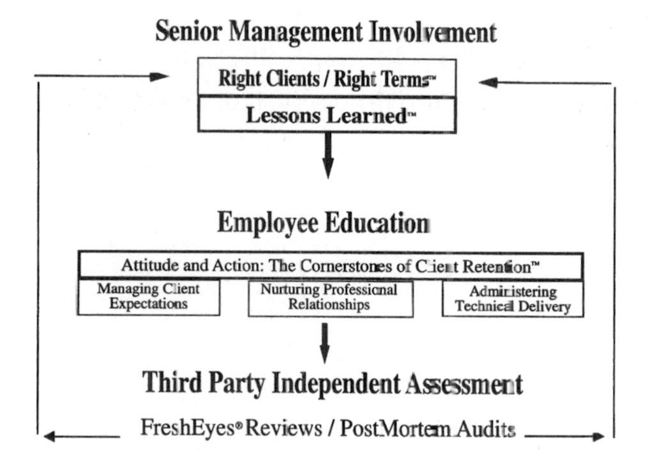

"There, now I can visualize the entire process," Bonnie thought to herself.

What Your Clients Won't Tell You...
And Your Managers Don't Know

"Beef or chicken?" the flight attendant asked.

"What?" Bonnie replied absently.

"You have your choice of beef or chicken for dinner," the attendant repeated in a friendly voice.

"Chicken, please," Bonnie replied as she put her notes away.

A meal, a movie and she'd be home. She couldn't wait to see her husband and hug her little ones.

Appendix

I. The Clients for Life Philosophy

A. Client retention is not a "program"; it's an ongoing commitment to your clients and colleagues.

II. Cornerstones of Client Retention

A. Attitude and Action are the cornerstones of the Clients for Life philosophy.

1. Attitude: We never lose a client that meets our criteria. We're proactive in helping the client solve problems and take advantage of opportunities.

2. Action: When and if we perceive a threat, we take whatever action is necessary to

protect the account.

B. Encouraging employees to assimilate this philosophy takes time—they must experience your commitment to become believers themselves.

C. All clients should be crucial to you or you shouldn't be doing business with them.

III. **Right Clients/Right Terms**

A. The senior executive and his or her staff is responsible for developing and later articulating the criteria that describe the "right clients" and detail the "right terms."

B. All senior managers should be involved in the following process:

Step 1: Ask the senior managers in attendance to think about and capture the "demographic and psychographic profile" of the "ideal" client.

Step 2: Ask the senior managers in attendance to share their descriptions one criteria at a time, going from person to person, until all the criteria are captured on flip charts and the sheets have been tacked up on the walls of the meeting room.

Step 3: Facilitate a discussion of the criteria. Look for early consensus. Explore conflicting experiences. Encourage debate among the attendees.

Step 4: Identify the "must have" criteria regarding the "right clients" that will not be violated—no matter how good the terms.

Step 5: Conduct the same process regarding the "right terms."

Note: The results should range from "10 to 12" demographic and psychographic criteria. These terms must be clearly articulated by the senior executive and interpreted consistently within the organization.

C. The Right Clients/Right Terms criteria should be reviewed every six months.

1. A change in key decision-makers is the most common reason to review an account.

D. When a client is no longer willing to do business under the "right terms," resigning an account is a proactive management decision.

1. It's more profitable to resign an account

that no longer fits your criteria than to continue to do business at unacceptable profit levels.

E. How you close a contract is as important as how you open one.

1. As soon as you decide to resign an account, devise an exit plan which doesn't divulge proprietary information but keeps the client's operation running.

2. An "official" closing takes place when the firms cease to do business under contract, but unofficial relationships can last a life time.

3. Stay in touch—keeping the personal contacts does take effort, but not as much effort as selling a new client from scratch.

4. Former clients can provide a constant source of leads and referrals.

IV. **Keeping What You've Worked So Hard to Get**

A. Client retention isn't an event. It's a daily process.

B. The worst possible time to renew a contract is when it's due for renewal. If you wait until then, you lose the incumbent's advantage.

C. Provided you've taken the right clients under the right terms, your responsibility is to protect the client's interests—which are the same as yours.

1. Protecting the client's interests dramatically reduces the likelihood of client confrontations.

2. When a confrontation does occur, its' focus is on the client's business, not on your firm's profits.

3. You must care enough to confront the client on issues of concern.

V. **Sharing the Lessons Learned**

A. Lessons Learned are the handful of reasons that explain the majority of the losses historically in curred.

1. Senior managers are responsible for identifying the lessons learned, communicating these lessons to their employees and sharing the tactics they've used to eliminate these threats.

2. Everyone is responsible for taking the action indicated by the senior managers when one of the threats presents itself.

B. When people change, everything has the potential to change.

1. A new client decision-maker might see things so differently as to no longer be the right client under the right terms.

VI. **Start-Up: A Crucial Time**

A. All managers should go through a sales and negotiating course to improve their skills when interacting with clients and with their own managers who influence the start-up process.

B. Always start up according to the client's expectations.

C. The Transition meeting is a process that must take place prior to of the start of a new contract.

D. Delay your own firm's SOP (Standard Operating Practices) if it creates a conflict with the client's expectations regarding the start-up.

1. Delaying your SOP does not mean de ceiving your own firm; it simply means using your talents to sell management on the need to be patient in implementing some of the required procedures.

VII. **The Transition Meeting**

A. This meeting's attendees include everyone in the client's decision-making unit and the service provider's sales rep, the operations manager responsible for implementing the contract, and the business unit manager ultimately responsible for the company's performance.

B. The Transition meeting also includes any new client decision-makers who have assumed responsibility since the signing of the contract.

C. All client participants write down their immediate, short-term, and long-term expectations.

D. These written statements become the basis for open discussion between firms.

E. In the unlikely event that the clients are unwilling to abide by the "right terms"—after exhausting all possible ways of finding a "win-win" solution—the discussion should shift to the creation of an exit plan*.

* Unless you are willing to walk away, you cannot

negotiate effectively.

VIII. **Sales and Operations: A Consistent Message and Mission**

A. Expect your clients to have expectations you didn't expect they would have—as long as those expectations don't violate the "right clients/right terms" criteria, that's OK.

B. Sales reps can't be expected to foresee all client expectations, but they must be responsible team members.

C. The Transition meeting is the vehicle that keeps sales people from promising more than operations can deliver.

1. Representatives from sales and operations

must attend the Transition meeting.

2. At the meeting, operations managers can refuse to accept the assignment.

3. No contract is valid until after the Transition meeting, which is the final stage of negotiations.

4. The contract's language must include the expectations of both companies and must specify that the Transition meeting will make all negotiations final.

5. Operations must not begin work without a signed contract.

6. No commissions should be paid to the sales staff until after a successful Transition meeting.

D. The notion that growth comes from your next client is a fallacy.

1. In an existing business of any size, to deliver the profit of one existing client takes at least three new clients of the same size.

2. Success depends not upon growth but upon **profitable** growth.

IX. **If you Leave Client Retention to Chance...**

A. If you leave client retention to chance, chances are you're going to lose clients. Client retention demands a formal process.

B. To avoid thirty percent of lost clients, educate your employees in three key areas:

1. Managing client expectations.

2. Developing relationships at all levels of both organizations....A web of influence.

3. Delivering the technical aspects of your service in a way that's consistent with the client's expectations.

C. To avoid twenty percent of lost clients, use an independent 3rd party to help access the status of your clients and contracts.

1. Customer satisfaction surveys don't work in a management services environment.

2. FreshEyes Reviews monitor current client satisfaction.

3. PostMortem Audits reveal reasons for client defections and help management avoid repeating mistakes.

X. **Managing Client Expectations**

A. The next thirty percent of potential losses can be saved by educating your managers. The first piece of information they need is how to understand and manage their clients' expectations.

B. Expectations are formed from prior personal experiences and all forms of communication—particularly those used during the selling process.

1. To judge our performance, clients use their expectations of what will happen and not what "really" happens.

2. Client expectations are constantly chang-

ing as clients have new experiences and are exposed to new communications.

3. By using the power of personal communications, it's possible to create, influence and manage client expectations, but not to control them.

4. The secret to understanding client expectations is to ASK.

    a. Ask your clients about their expectations on a quarterly basis to stay in touch with client needs, reinforce your value to the client and obtain funding or approvals for future projects.

C. When dealing with clients, deliver superior performance, but beware of the Expectations Paradox.

What Your Clients Won't Tell You...
And Your Managers Don't Know

1. Clients for Life defines superior performance as performance that exceeds the client's expectations.

2. Exceed the expectation, but by just a little or suffer the consequences of the Expectations Paradox.

3. The Expectations Paradox strikes when you provide the client with experiences that you can not deliver consistently.

4. Clients will accept the service provider's limits under three conditions:

a. The client trusts you.

b. The limits are real.

c. The competition can't do better.

XI. **Nurturing Professional Relationships**

A. Like personal relationships, professional relationships flourish when they're based on trust and respect.

1. Trust is created by consistently demonstrating candor, competency, and concern.

2. Trust takes a long time to build but a split second to lose.

3. Respect is gained when you take a stand on the things people know are right.

B. Always weave and maintain a Web of Influence.

1. Never let the contract depend on one business* relationship, no matter how high in the client's organization.

* A business relationships means that your client knows you, trusts and respects you and will meet with you—provided you have a valid business reason for meeting.

2. Every one of our managers must be tied to three in the client's organization.

C. Create a database of information on each client.

1. This information should include the client's home town, college attended, marital status, anniversary date, spouse's name, home address and phone number, children's names and ages, hobbies, favorite restau-

rants, clubs and associations, etc.

2. A database like this is crucial to maintaining client relationships as people transfer within the company or leave to pursue their own careers.

XII. **Solving Problems and Delivering Innovation**

A. From a technical standpoint, clients expect a services provider to solve their problems and bring innovation to their business.

1. The key to solving a client's problems is agreement on what the problems are and understanding the priorities the client assigns to getting them fixed.

2. Innovation is something clients are not yet doing for themselves.

3. Innovation need not be a newly acquired skill to be a revelation to the client.

B. Document your successes; your failures will document themselves.

1. Documentation of success will leave a paper trail beneficial to your organization in times of change.

XIII. **The FreshEyes® Review and the PostMortem Audit™**

A. Both of these processes must be done by unbiased, third-party individuals or organizations or the information may not only be suspect but truly counterproductive. Advanced and highly developed probing, listening and writing skills are required to elicit, verifiy and communicate what is learned. Action must be taken based on the information each of the processes provides.

B. The FreshEyes Review should be conducted annually at all key accounts and/or when a significant event or change occurs for a client.

1. The FreshEyes Review asks these questions:

a. How are we living up to the client's expectations?

b. How good are the relationships between the people representing the organizations?

c. How effective is the delivery of our technical services?

C. A PostMortem Audit should be conducted within

two months of the time the contract is canceled.

1. PostMortem Audits ask these questions:

   a. Where did we fail to live up to the client's expectations?

   b. Where did our Web of Influence break down?

   c. Where did the technical aspects of our service fall short?

D. Mistakes can be corrected only after they've been acknowledged.

E. To reinforce your value to a new client, engage in the Transition Lite process. Review with the client the condition of the business when you first assumed responsibility for the account, its condition now, and the clients expectations for the future.